Challenge of the Sea

by

Yocky Lol Gilson

DORRANCE PUBLISHING CO., INC.
PITTSBURGH, PENNSYLVANIA 15222

All Rights Reserved
Copyright © 2009 by Yocky Lol Gilson
No part of this book may be reproduced or transmitted
in any form or by any means, electronic or mechanical,
including photocopying, recording, or by any information
storage and retrieval system without permission in
writing from the author.

ISBN: 978-1-4349-0185-9
Library of Congress Control Number: 2008941588

Printed in the United States of America

First Printing

For information or to order additional books, please write:
Dorrance Publishing Co., Inc.
701 Smithfield St.
Pittsburgh, Pennsylvania 15222
U.S.A.
1-800-788-7654
www.dorrancebookstore.com

Dedication

To an excellent mother and father, who should have thrown me away when I was one very sick, horrible little boy.

To my devoted wife, who never complained about the long hours, weeks, and years she was left to cope with the family on her own.

To my wider family, who always manage to rally round when the going gets tough.

Thanks to my friend Mike Wilson, for all his backup.

To the memory of an inshore fishing industry that may soon be forgotten, and my father, W.E. Gilson, MBE, who never tired of working for his family.

Perhaps the greatest battle was fought over and around the Thames Estuary and the English Channel, taking in the counties of Essex, Kent, and Sussex. This left the seabed littered with sunken ships, fighter and bomber planes that had been blown to pieces, unexploded mines, rockets, bombs, and live shells of every description. Much of this has been lifted with the trawl and cleared away by trawler men during the course of their normal fishing.

Introduction

My story begins sometime around the turn of the eighteenth century. It could well have commenced two hundred years earlier. But doubt about definite fact and questionable details available from that period of our family history, way back in the past, would make it somewhat vague, to say the least. I will endeavour to give my readers just an outline of our lowly beginnings.

If our information is even close to the truth, It would appear that our ancestors came from either Belgium or Holland in the latter part of the sixteenth century. Having landed in England, they established themselves on either side of the Thames estuary, mainly in Kent and Essex. They were professional fishermen and part-time smugglers. They fished when it was lucrative but would regularly run contraband across the English Channel in order to subsidise their earnings. It was all part of a way of life and a very exciting one, to say the least.

This book contains many stories that I have related to listeners from all walks of life. It is at the insistence of these people that I am attempting to write down the true experiences of a family of very ordinary fishermen over the last one hundred and fifty years. This is as close to the actual fact as one can get.

Many romantic stories have been written down through the ages about the sea and men that go down to the sea in ships: voyages of discovery and exploration, great sea battles, pirates and smugglers risking life and limb to avoid capture by the Navy or Customs and excise, knowing that brutal floggings and imprisonment were waiting for them if they were unlucky enough to be caught.

Having been born into a family of fishermen who descended from a long line of fishermen come smugglers, I had always boasted that if I were to survive and live into retirement I would attempt to write a book—never believing that this could possibly happen. My life as a fisherman has been somewhat perilous.

Even now as I sit writing these words it is difficult to associate myself with all the wonderful, dangerous, exciting, funny, and most unlikely happenings over fifty years connected with the sea and fishing. Did all these adventures really take place? Is is it possible for me, a fisherman all my working life, to tell and capture the excitement of so many experiences, which even now are so vivid and alive in my memory? I am going to try.

My father, William Gilson (nicknamed Yocky) looked at me with as much ferocity on his face as he could muster. "Your biggest problem, Loll, is you are too much like your great-uncle George." That's where my story begins. I was twelve years of age.

A Brief Explanation

In order to give readers of this book a better understanding of the type of fisherman that I became over the years, I am going to try to explain the different nets that I made and fished with over a period of forty years. If I talk about gear, that means the net and all the surrounding attachments that go into making a net usable.

Saying that a person is a fisherman means very little to anyone, due to the fact that there are so many different applications a person can use in the process of catching fish.

It is quite feasible for a person to catch fish throughout their life and never go near a boat of any sort, never mind about going to sea.

As a fisherman that has learnt the art of fishing in the Thames Estuary and the English Channel, I have always considered that I was privileged to experience most of the different types of gear that contribute to making a fisherman aware of most if not all of the possibilities.

Most types of gear have a totally different application when worked in dead water as opposed to working with a hard running tide. The colour of the water changes. The habits of the fish change, sometimes beyond all recognition, often in clear water making the fish almost uncatchable. I am going to name the types of gear that I have worked over the years and then try to explain.

I have never considered myself to be an expert on line (hook) fishing but because my father worked what we called band lines during the second world war, this is where my life as a fisherman began.

First we would walk off on the mud at Southend-on-Sea and dig the worms for bait. Then, when the hooks had been baited, we would walk off again and anchor the band lines on the foreshore while the tide was out. My father preferred to lay the lines just as the tide was flowing. This decreased the chances of catching seagulls. Then we would walk off as the tide ebbed and remove the fish from the five hundred hooks. One of the favourite spots was Thorpe-bay near the Beach huts. This was also one of the few places that gave access through the barbed wire and tank traps which made up the sea defence. It was somewhat laborious but it often provided a day's pay, if the weather was bad. In winter it would often yield several cod and one or two boxes of plaice and flounders—not a lot, but it helped. I usually finished up selling these round the houses, retail. I was twelve years old.

I did work band lines (long-lines) on a few occasions in the English Channel, fishing for turbot and skate and using two thousand hooks. But this was only a stand-by, not on a regular basis.

Another method that was used during the war was hoop-net fishing. This involved a metal hoop with a net stocking attached underneath, with double wires criss-crossed on the hoop (to hold the bait) and a tripod made up of thin rod on which the pulling rope was fastened. The hoop was lowered to the sea-bed and held slightly off the bottom.

Conditions for Hoop-net fishing needed to be almost perfect to achieve even a modicum of success. The fish also had to be very plentiful, which indeed they were during and just after the war.

My father always maintained that there was an art in striking (snatching off the sea-bed) a hoop-net and I have no doubt that there was. It was obvious that, as in all types of fishing, some were far more successful than others. This was often referred to as luck but I don't believe that is true. In most cases it is application.

My grandfather had a reputation of being a top drag-net fisherman. He certainly built up a considerable trade for eels, mullet, and smelts (cucumber fish), These were at that time all caught in a drag-net worked off of the different sand banks in the Thames estuary, Once again, conditions had to be favourable.

Much of the skill of being a successful fisherman in the old days came from experience, a great deal of flair and a lot of guess-work. This was very evident in the success or failure of the old stow-boaters when fishing for sprats, herrings, and whitebait.

When the last of the stow-boat fishing was coming to an end, my brother Peter worked on board the stow boat with Sam Thomas. At the same time we were experimenting with a trawl for the purpose of catching sprats. Little did we realize at the time that there would come a day in the not too distant future when we would use a pelagic trawl on certain tides to catch almost everything, in fact multipurpose.

Before the days of echo sounders and fish finders, it was a case of following the birds that were feeding on the fish, guessing at what depth the sprats were swimming, and hoping that the net was capable of catching them. In that first season we made and modified thirteen trawls.

The stow-boats anchored and depended on the tide. With a trawl we were able to follow the fish around but without an echo sounder there was still a great deal of guess-work. Years of experience helped a lot in all methods of fishing. In this day and age, most of this can be taught in a classroom. I am quite certain that with the knowledge I possessed at the end of my working life, I could have retired at the tender age of twenty, a very rich man and without all the bruises.

One day in particular stands out in my mind above all others. This was a day when the old and the new came together in one huge bonanza, It was a day to remember for the record books.

We were in the most unusual position of being able to choose between several different large shoals of fish. One cannery that was purchasing our sprats wanted all large fish, no more than sixty-eight to the kilo, which is indeed a large sprat for the Thames estuary and no discard.

One area of the fishery was yielding fish of this size but only on certain tides. We decided that we would sample some of the shoals further from home.

We had made one haul in the North Swin of no more than ten minutes. The fish were so plentiful that we caught ten ton and had to slip them (throw them away) because they were too small.

We then moved across into the Barrow deeps where it was obvious that on the low water there would be an abundance of sprats, but would they be big enough? There were gathering in the area two of the old stow-boaters and seven pair of pelagic trawlers, all with echo sounders. It was a beautiful day with conditions perfect for any type of sprat fishing.

Seagulls were going mad as they fed on the enormous shoals of fish, At times it was impossible to see through the gulls and they stretched for several miles. They were feeding on the fish close to the surface, which are normally the small. A dozen seals were having a birthday feast.

There were also more than twenty gannet (large white birds), These were diving down several feet under the surface and feeding on the larger fish. On the echo sounder the fish were showing almost top to bottom in twelve-fathom depth of water. I had never seen such a concentration of fish over such a large area. They were all gathering around the Mid-Barrow lightship but spread over an enormous area. Thousands of tons of sprats and good quality, but not large enough for the big fish contract. They would have to go to the other two canneries.

All the boats filled their fish-holds and some even filled the decks as well. It was just as well that it was a flat calm; in any other weather this would have been out of the question. It was a very special day and a day for the history books. Even the two stow-boaters were full.

Before heading for home, we collected letters from the Mid-Barrow lightship and gave them all the newspapers and magazines that we had on board, This was a custom that we always carried out whenever we were close to the lightships or gun forts. We gave them plenty of fish and they were always more than pleased to see us. In those days it was a pretty lonely existence for the crews that manned them.

All but one of the stow-boats had gone out of commission, the last one being a vessel called the Saxonia. She fished specifically for whitebait and only continued for a short period of time after the war ended.

Beam trawling for shrimps, which Father had always insisted was our bread and butter, soon became outdated. This was one of the most frustrating fisheries, mainly because there were far too many vessels involved and the bulk of the catch went into the London market. The outlet was never sufficient to cater for the catching ability of quite a large fleet.

We changed the grounds that we fished constantly in our efforts to vary the mixture of shrimps and fish that could be caught with a beam trawl. We made regular trips down to the Queen's Channel and had some wonderful catches of pink shrimps, But it was a fishery that was doomed to failure. It was not a fishery that one could confidently invest any amount of money in long-term. The otter trawl for mixed fish quickly began to take over, much to Father's disgust.

The Peter-net fishing also began to wind down towards closure. It had been a very popular fishery during and for ten years after the end of the war. Shooting the twelve fifteen-fathom-long nets across the tide in shallow water on both sides of the Thames estuary had been a huge success, while there was an abundance of skate and plaice.

I had fished with the Peter nets in all the guts and dreans from the South Shoebury Buoy down to the Whittaker beacon on the North side and from Scraps-gate down to Whitstable Street on the South side, It was a great fishery in its time but was doomed in the face of new methods and more powerful vessels.

When I look back over the years and remember all the changes that have taken place, I think about those freezing cold mornings in an open boat without protection of any sort whatsoever and wonder how I survived. It was certainly good experience—but a very hard way to learn.

My first fishing voyage in the real world was at the the tender age of eleven, in an under-twenty-foot open skiff in the middle of winter, totally without protection from the bitterly cold northerly winds, The trip lasted more than twelve hours and we were fishing for cod. From that moment in time I was made fully aware that all fishermen have a pretty hard life, especially so in the Thames estuary—the lifeline of London—and out into the English channel and southern North Sea. It was halfway through the second world war and the numbers of ships wrecked, moored, or actually under way were a constant menace. The amount of debris from aircraft destroyed in the area plus the rubbish dumped by hundreds of ships moored in the estuary preparing for the Normandy landings was unbelievable and a constant danger to all fishermen. Perhaps if I had known at the time that I would devote a considerable part of my fishing life to clearing up the mess that was being created by war, I might not have been quite so keen. But there have been very few dull moments in my life and I have no regrets.

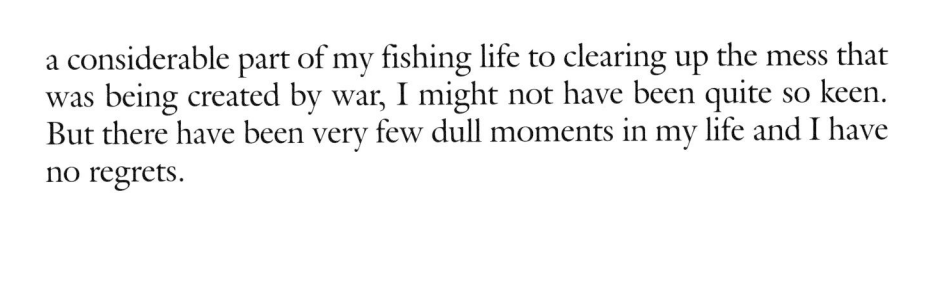

Prologue

The tiny vessel literally forced her way down the English channel against a howling storm, force-ten gale.

Coast guards following her progress through binoculars expressed the opinion that whoever was skippering the sturdy little ship had to be ignorant or completely mad,

All cross-channel ferries had ceased their activities several hours before. The weather was diabolical, and that was putting it rather mildly. Was it possible that she could survive in such atrocious conditions? The coast guards were doubtful.

Being the skipper of the Dor-Bet, I was concerned but not unduly worried. She was awash most of the time but kept coming up for more, and although some of the wheelhouse joints were weeping it had all happened many times before. I was treading that thin, marginal line that separated the successful fishermen from the mentally unbalanced, and I accepted the risk as part of my life.

My name is Laurie Gilson and I come from a long line of fishermen-cum-smugglers. I am a hunter. There were fish to be caught and I intended to be in the right place at the right time to catch them. My choices had been made earlier in the day; turning back was not a consideration.

The entrance to Dover Harbour and the smooth waters beyond were almost in sight. The safety of that sheltered basin ahead meant that I would be within two hours' steam of the fishing grounds I intended to work later, if the weather improved. So much depended on that little word: *If.*

1

I was twenty-seven years of age, having been born in nineteen thirty-one. The Dor-Bet was only two years old and I had been her skipper since the day she was launched. *The world is my oyster and the sea belongs to me,* at least that's what I think at this moment of time. Naturally, during the course of my extremely long life as a sea-going fisherman, I was going to find out that this is not quite how the world works but at this point in my fishing experience, life was very good.

I left school at the age of fourteen and had been to sea with my father and brothers many times before this. I was always going to be a fisherman!, even at the tender age of six, eventually becoming skipper of my father's boat just before my eighteenth birthday. The vessel that I took command of was named the Reindeer, so called because she was reputed to be the fastest sailing cockle boat in the fleet at the time she was built. Having a centre board and a full set of sails, she was one of the last fishing boats in the area to be built without an engine installed; this came later. My father sold the Reindeer when the Dor-Bet was launched.

Having watched and waited for the Dor-Bet to be built, I found it one of the most exciting days of my life when she was launched. The coming of the Dor-Bet enabled me to spread my wings and fish outside the Thames estuary, into the English

Channel and the North Sea. I had dreamed about these things for many years and most of my dreams were being realized.

Steaming down the English Channel towards Dover in a force-ten gale is not what one would call a picnic. Neither is it very comfortable, but it is exciting.

In my mind is the thought of the mixture of prime fish that are waiting to be caught on the right grounds at the right time. If the wind drops away.

With a little bit of luck (which all fishermen need), in twenty minutes we shall be in the smooth waters of Dover Harbour. We are bound for Hythe Bay, west of Folkestone. But because of the amount of wind, we will be compelled to take a breather.

I am very surprised and also concerned to see that the no-entry signals are flying on the harbour entrance. It would appear that the cross-channel ferries have ceased to operate. This is the first time I have ever seen the no-entry signal flying, certainly not the welcome I was hoping for. The Dor-Bet has been punching a full-blown gale for several hours. My mate Fred and I need to get a few hours' rest if we are to be fit for a long day's trawling on the following day.

It is with some considerable relief that we see the signals change. We steam gratefully past the coast guard's station into the calm waters of the harbour. The coast guard's greeting was to put one hand over his mouth and one finger to the side of his head. He did not appear to be amused.

The Dor-Bet is thirty-six feet in length and eleven feet six inches wide, with a draught of four feet. Built of Canadian pine on solid oak-frame timbers, she was just a small in-shore fishing boat, but because I had served much of my early fishing days in much smaller vessels, to me she was really something quite special—even if the crew did consist only of myself as skipper, and Fred Emery, my mate, right-hand man, and close friend.

Fred had been a Leigh-on-Sea cockle fisherman before joining me to replace one of my brothers who now owned and skippered his own vessel. It had taken me quite some time to get used to working with Fred, who measured more than six feet tall, compared to my own five feet eight inches at a stretch. He was big-boned and inclined to be rather loud, always speaking his mind no matter where or what the situation. Irrespective of who happened to be present at the time, Fred always spoke his piece. He also had the reputation of being the top gatherer of hand-raked cockles in the trade, and he would tell you so. I had not the slightest doubt that it was true. He had proved to me many times over the last two years that he was prepared to work until he dropped, which was something we both had in common. This bond bound us close together. We had become a very efficient working unit, and enjoyed our fishing life together.

We berthed alongside the very high harbour wall. Fred had quickly run up the steep steps and dropped the ropes over the bollards provided. He straightened up and came face to face with one very irate harbourmaster, who accused him of having taken leave of his senses. Fred responded in his usual loud, abrupt fashion, "Don't blame me, Captain, tell the skipper, but tell him from a distance—he is inclined to be a bit of a firecracker when roused." This was one of Fred's typical wind-ups. I laughed and invited the harbourmaster aboard for a cup of tea, which he accepted. We soon became friends. I explained that we were only taking shelter until the wind died away a little; all being well, we would be sailing in the early hours of the morning. He expressed his doubts about the wind dropping so soon, but wished us well and left us in peace. For this I was quite grateful; I was expecting him to bring up the question of harbour dues. I am never very keen on parting with money, especially prior to earning some.

We had to tidy the ship, eat, sleep, and prepare the fishing gear for the next day. I always kept three complete sets of trawl gear on the deck ready to use. Experience had taught me always to be prepared for the worst, as damage to the working trawl was unavoidable, It was quicker more often than not to change gear rather than mend, The mending could be carried out at a later date. Making the most of the time at sea was and always will be of the utmost importance. The previous year, on my first voyage down channel, while learning the nature of the ground and how to keep clear of the wrecks not marked on the chart, my netting needle seldom left my hand. Every spare moment was used keeping the gear intact. Sleep and food were secondary.

The Dor-Bet had been designed for work, not comfort. Galley and sleeping accommodations situated right forward in the bows behind the Samson post allowed very little room to move about, especially when one had a mate the size of Fred. It was a bit cramped, to say the least. The distance from the stem to the first bulkhead is just a short ten feet, behind which the one-hundred-brake horsepower engine is installed. The sides of the engine room are cut diagonal to increase carrying capacity.

In the wintertime, when we are fishing for sprats and herring, the fish are pushed forward from the fish hold, allowing the little vessel to carry an unbelievable ten tons maximum. The Dor-Bet could only be loaded to this extent in very fine weather and calm sea conditions and these are winter fish. We are at this moment of time in the middle of summer, hunting Dover soles, plaice, skate, and anything else that swims in front of the gear as we tow the trawl along the sea-bed.

Fred has got the frying pan on the little liquid gas cooker and the smell of bacon is wafting up from the cabin. I realize that it is some ten hours since we last had anything to eat, and look forward to a good fry-up and some sleep. When we are in harbour we try to make an occasion of going ashore for a meal but we are restricted for time. It is almost eight o'clock in the evening and I intend to be steaming towards the fishing grounds west of Folkestone at four A.M. tomorrow morning, We need to get turned in as soon as possible.

The meal is quickly disposed of and Fred is soon snoring. Having checked that all is well on deck, I settle down to join him but as always, before I drop off to sleep plans for the next day's fishing run through my mind. That's if the wind drops away.

I have never quite understood how it works but at three A.M the following morning I stop the alarm clock from waking Fred. The clock in my mind usually brings me up on deck before the waking call comes. This morning I breathe a sigh of relief at finding that the wind has decreased considerably. There is still a fresh breeze and a heavy swell running but, providing the wind continues to drop away, the swell will gradually ease.

Fred is rudely awakened from his slumbers and in less than thirty minutes the Dor-Bet is once again crashing head first into the white-topped waves. Fred is not amused.

It was becoming increasingly clear that I had been more than a little optimistic in assuming that the very heavy swell would quickly ease away. We are now only ten minutes' steaming time east of Folkestone Harbour and there is no sign of the local fishermen making a move to put to sea. This is my third season working the Channel and I have become good friends with some of them. Bert Reed, Val Noakes, La La, Brickle are all top men of their chosen profession and would be out to fish as soon as they considered the weather fit. We had motored the first half-hour in the half-light but it is now broad daylight and the sky looks a murky grey colour. In fact it has just started to rain. Not a bit like summer, and certainly not the weather I was hoping for.

Just as it began to look likely that we would have to put into Folkestone and once again seek shelter, the wind shifted. In just the blink of an eye the southwest wind veered northwest, changing the whole situation. We now had an off-shore wind as opposed to an on-shore wind. It continued to blow quite fresh but if it continued in a northwesterly direction? Then we could look forward to a reasonably comfortable day. The swell would quickly disappear.

The gear is all ready to be shot away. We are twenty minutes west of Folkestone Harbour and the landmarks I have taken in previous years come into line. The Dor-Bet turns full circle in order to shoot away for the first time this voyage. The excitement begins to stir at the thought of fish coming aboard but we still have to wait a while yet.

The Dor-Bet is what is known in the fishing industry as a sidewinder. The vessel turns full circle in order to shoot the net over the side. As the vessel comes back on her original course the winch brakes are gradually released and the otter boards are paid away until the whole of the gear is firmly on the seabed. The towing wires are then brought into line astern and fixed into the stern rollers. At last we have commenced to fish.

We are towing along the seabed at between two and three knots and will continue to do so for about one and a half hours: if all goes well.

Fred prepares the deck for when the fish start coming aboard and then goes down into the galley to make a cup of tea. This is what a fisherman's life is all about. All the discomfort and rigorous exercise that we have endured in the last twenty-four hours are all for this moment. My fingers are crossed and I say a little word. We must catch plenty of fish.

The gear I keep referring to consists of two otter boards (port and starboard) plus fifteen fathoms of sweep chain leading to the heavier end chains, which are two fathoms in length, Then a nine-fathom ground chain to which the net is secured. The net is a standard nine-fathom otter trawl, sometimes factory-made, more often than not hand-netted. Two of the three nets on deck at the present moment I hand-netted. It's a great hobby if you need to meditate.

We are now trawling in the five-fathom line west of Folkestone Harbour. It is my intention to maintain this depth of water for roughly an hour and then to deepen the water off into the seven-fathom line for the last part of the haul. I have checked the marks on the towing wires just to confirm that the gear is firmly on the seabed (twenty fathoms on the stern) and that the gear is spread to its maximum width. It is always possible that there can be a foul-up of some sort as the gear sinks to the seabed but thankfully everything looks normal. More from habit than from necessity I put my hand on the towing wire, just to satisfy myself that the otter boards are running smoothly along the seabed and confirming that the ground has not changed a great deal from the previous year that I fished here. The five-fathom line has always consisted of nice soft smooth sand, ideal for the type of gear we are using.

I can smell that Fred is making toast for breakfast. The small gas stove in the galley has just two hobs and a grill, not very sophisticated but it suits our purposes. The closest we ever get to a banquet is a good fry-up or a crab or lobster salad, which is a meal we enjoy quite often. Just one of the fringe benefits of being a poor fisherman.

When we are trawling on ground for the first time in a season I like to concentrate on the echo sounder. It will not show any small objects on the seabed but it will show me if there have been any drastic changes since I fished on this ground the last time. In most cases when we suffer damage to the nets, it is seldom that we find the actual cause. It might be just an old tin can sticking up from the seabed, but I have picked up enough rubbish in my time at sea to fill a scrap yard or, in many cases, a museum.

Looking astern towards Folkestone and in an easterly direction where the sun has just started to show through the clouds, I can see that several of the local fleet are now coming out of the harbour. There are bound to be some rude remarks that I am trespassing on someone's freehold.

In the three seasons that I have been working the channel, the local fishermen have received me very well but my own brothers are never happy if when coming to sea very early in the morning they find a stranger fishing on their doorstep. It is a bit hard to swallow. We shall soon find out. La La is coming alongside and will soon be in hailing distance. He puts his head out of the wheelhouse window and enquires: what I am doing on his Fluffing ground!. (At least I think he said fluffing) but he has a big grin on his face so I am inclined to think that for the present moment all is well.

We have just altered course slightly in a southerly direction and this is gradually taking the Dor-Bet further away from the shelter of the land, which is now the best part of a mile away. But the wind is now broad off the land and working conditions as near perfect as they get. At the present moment there is plenty of colour in the water, which has been well and truly stirred up by the gale continuing throughout the night. Bearing these conditions in mind I am hoping that this first haul will yield more soles than normal for this particular piece of ground. Once the swell dies down and the water clears the soles usually disappear until the dark fishing. When night comes we shall move back into the more shallow water, sometimes as close to the land as we can possibly get. This is often where the larger top-quality soles tend to hang out, but they swim much too fast for the Dor-Bet to keep up with them when the water is clear. We have to bide our time.

On this first haul of our trip down-channel I have my fingers crossed in the hope that we are going to catch a mixture of large plaice and soles. This area of ground we are working seldom yields any amount of small fish. We are not expecting a large bulk of fish, just good quality and perhaps the odd lobster or crab. The excitement begins to mount as Fred prepares the winch for hauling. This is the moment we have been waiting for. The moment of truth.

One otter board comes out of the water and up to the gallows amidships. The other comes up to the stern roller. The Dor-Bet now lies side to the wind and down wind of the gear, not moving apart from the steady roll. Fred takes the after stern sweep and begins to pull. I do the same amid-ships. If there is too much weight we transfer the sweeps to the winch. This takes more time and is a move only carried out if absolutely necessary.

At last the sweeps and the end chains are aboard. It's a good pull but we are both used to the exercise and often pretend it's a race to see who can get to the middle of the ground chain first. We then each take one side of the net (which is called the selvage) and keep pulling until we reach the cod-end.

Already we have seen several large plaice sliding down the net and as we come to the cod-end we pull the selvages together. Fred is grinning and his tongue is hanging out (Fred's tongue always hangs out when he gets excited). We hoist the cod-end aboard and release the fish onto the deck. It looks good. In fact it looks very good.

My father was possibly one of the most conservation-minded fishermen of his time. As soon as the net came aboard and there were fish on the deck he would insist on quickly carrying out a rough sorting operation in order to get the small fish back into the water as soon as possible, while they were still alive. Hands, feet, pieces of wood, and even wooden shovels were used to push the unwanted fish through the scuppers and back into the sea. Naturally many of the discarded fish are eaten by the seagulls but many of them survive and live to keep the stocks healthy. Today we don't have that problem.

The Dor-Bet has been gradually drifting away from the land and off into deeper water. I check the echo sounder to find that we are now almost off to the eleven-fathom line (sixty-six-foot depth of water). I check the landmarks just to make absolutely certain that we are in the right line. And once again we shoot the net away.

During the years I have been learning my trade, keeping landmarks and dead reckoning compass courses have saved me a great deal of grief and torn nets. On this haul we shall be towing on marks I had taken in previous years and I shall be keeping the east point of Folkestone harbour on a mast that is situated on the top of the cliffs, down towards Dover. This line had yielded some very good fishing in the past and also kept me clear of any wrecks or rough ground that would be likely to damage the net.

Fred puts the winch brakes on and once again we are towing the seabed. This haul we have the thirty-fathom mark on the stern. Deeper water, more towing wire; the gear must be firmly on the bottom. I tell Fred to pay away another five fathoms just to make sure. Then we turn our attention to clearing and sorting the different species of fish into boxes. There is hardly any discard at all and most of the four stone of soles and seven stone of plaice are top-quality. Fred makes the comment, "Real prime." But there are also different types of fish which are just as desirable. Three nice lobsters. Several eating crabs, one in particular that has probably been in a fight at some time in his life and has had the misfortune to lose a claw. "That one goes in the pot for dinner tomorrow," says Fred with a big, toothy grin. There are also several lemon soles, a fourteen-pound turbot, and a beautifully marked eight-pound brill.

I just check and make certain that the Dor-Bet is on the correct course and staying in the right line. Fred has already started gutting the soles and I will help him as much as possible, just so long as the vessel keeps towing in the correct line. The weather is now ideal for our purposes and a small adjustment on the steering wheel (now and again) is all that is required to keep the little vessel going in the right direction. This tow will last somewhat longer than the first, for two and a half hours. If all goes well we should have the first haul all gutted and washed, boxed, and off the deck, and still have time for a cup of tea before the next haul comes aboard. *If* all goes well.

Looking at the quality of the fish in the boxes and the size of the Dover sole twisting and turning in Fred's hands in its attempt to escape the knife, I am sorely tempted to return to the more shallow waters where we carried out the first tow. But experience has taught me that with the water clearing and the tide dropping (ebbing), the ground will not yield a second time. I decide to carry out my planned routine for the day. It is always best to have a plan.

As the day proceeded my plan almost worked to perfection, but not quite. We made four tows in the next fourteen hours in and around the eleven-fathom line, each haul bringing us closer to Dungeness Point where the ground always appeared to be more rough. In all, the four tows yielded more than forty stone of marketable plaice and ten stone of mixed smaller fish, plaice, sand dabs, brill, and lemon sole, plus several spotted dogfish and three larger spur dogs, and five medium-sized skate, each weighing around the six-pound mark. These are all good money-making fish on the Folkestone market, where our catch will be landed tomorrow morning. If all goes well. One thing that I did not plan and could well have done without: We snagged the net on something that must have been quite sharp. It had ripped the net in three places from one side of the net to the other (in fisherman's language, from selvage to selvage). Fortunately this had happened on the last of the four tows in the deep water, a couple of hours before I planned to move back in closer to the land for the dark fishing. But because of the damage we were now forced to change nets, and I would have several hours of net repairing as soon as the time became available. Fred and I decided this would be a good time to heave-to for a couple of hours and have some dinner. We had almost managed to keep pace with the gutting and washing of the last four hauls and the deck was more or less clear. Fred thinks we have earned a little break.

I have learned many new things from coming down-Channel to work. Fishermen out of Folkestone call the small fish storkers. These are sold on the market as job lots. The storkers are not gutted. Money made from the sale of the storkers is shared out among the crew as perks. This also includes the dogfish, which appear to sell well on the market. When we are working in the Thames estuary we call the small fish hoppers. They are gutted, washed, and boxed in the same fashion as the rest of the catch, and is all part and parcel of the vessel's earnings. Dogfish I have often caught by the hundred, but unless we have the time and patience to skin them there would be no demand. This made it quite a nice bonus to be able to put them directly on the market, not even having to gut them. All these things run through my mind while I sit enjoying an egg and bacon sandwich Fred has prepared for me while I have been changing the gear. In another hour it will be dusk and we shall move in close to the land, near the block-ship and in as little as one fathom of water. With a little bit of luck, we shall be chasing the soles until day-light returns tomorrow morning. I should explain: The local fishermen call it the block-ship; Fred and I know it as the Mulbury Harbour.

Many times during the Second World War I had been to sea with my father and experienced all sorts of adventures. We had observed all the preparations for the invasion of France, the build-up of ships and men being made ready for the Normandy beach-head. The (block-ships) or Mulbury Harbours were all part of this operation, they were constructed of reinforced cement and placed at strategic points in the Thames estuary and the English Channel in readiness to be towed across to France to form a man-made artificial harbour to provide protection for the landing forces. Some of the block-ships never reached their destination. One in particular was wrongly positioned on a sand bank east of Southend-on-Sea Pier, broke into two pieces, and remains there to this day.

Just before dusk, we steamed in towards the block-ship that had been beached and left in Hythe Bay. I have no idea why it was not used for the invasion, as it appeared to be in perfectly good condition, but it certainly gave us a good mark to work with, even in the dark it stood out quite clearly, a black, ominous lump.

It is my intention to work just to the seaward side of the block-ship. As the daylight fades we shoot the gear away and start to trawl the seabed in a two-fathom depth of water. The ground in this area is relatively clear of trouble (or was). I am hoping for a nice quiet, comfortable night of fishing with plenty of soles and no nasty unwanted incidents. There is plenty of room to work without towing over the same ground twice. If the soles are here and all goes according to plan we shall make three hauls, which will take us through until daylight tomorrow morning. If all goes well.

The night quickly passes away and the net is coming aboard for the first haul. There are several sole stickers in the meshes and the signs look very promising. We have been towing for three hours and I am hoping for a good haul, seven or eight stone would be very acceptable. But if all the weight as we pull up on the selvages is anything to go on, there could be a great deal more.

We put the tackle hoist on the hoisting strop and Fred heaves up on the winch dolly. The cod-end swings aboard and it's a very big bag, all sheer soles, no rubbish whatsoever. It looks like a really bumper haul.

As it turns out, there are lots of small soles (slips and tonges, we call them), but there are fourteen stone of good savable soles, which makes for an excellent start to the nights fishing. We stop to sort the catch and push the small soles through the scuppers and overboard. Hopefully, most of them will survive and grow into parent stock for the future. But when a fish is small and unprotected the sea is a mighty dangerous place to live. We shoot the net away for our second haul and with a little bit of luck this will take us through until daylight returns. Always we need that little bit of luck.

In close to the land where we are now fishing, it is almost a flat calm. There is still a slight breeze which will almost certainly freshen in the early morning, but the night's trawling has been just about as good as it comes. The second haul has yielded well, although not quite as well as the first. We now have roughly twenty-five stone of soles ready to land on the market, two hours from now. All has gone very well.

We are on the last haul of the day, towing east towards Folkestone Harbour, and we have moved back off into the deeper water once more. The water is very clear and the tide is almost dead. I am hoping that we may catch a few more plaice and maybe a couple of boxes of mixed fish. There certainly won't be any soles. The water is as clear as gin, a term often used by fishermen to describe poor trawling conditions. It would appear that most if not all of the local boats went further to the west into the next bay for the night fishing. It will be some time before they land; we should be able to put our fish on the market and get out of their way before they come home. Not having a skiff in which to take our fish ashore, we have to go in alongside the slipway. We don't want to create any confusion. Fred puts the winch in gear and the net comes up for the last time on this trip. We have now been on the move for nearly thirty hours.

As we stow the gear and make our way into the harbour Fred appears to be taking a keen interest in a motorboat that is side to the wind and drifting out to sea about a mile from the land, The wind is now getting fresh once more. Fred thinks they might be in some kind of trouble. He has been watching the little boat for some time. If they have got problems and drift out too far from the land, they are going to find it very uncomfortable. I suggest he keep an eye on them until after we have put our fish on the market. Then we will have another look, check, and make sure they are okay.

In spite of the fact that this is the third year that I have been landing fish on the Folkestone market it still comes as a refreshing novelty. To actually stand and listen to the merchants bidding at the auction for the fish that we have just caught only a few hours before brings a great sense of satisfaction of a job well done and completed. Just twenty minutes and we know exactly what our efforts of the last thirty hours have yielded money-wise. So different from the marketing in our own port and in a family situation, where the catch from all the five vessels that belong to the family are lumped together and my father is responsible for the marketing. It is much more complicated and I never quite know how much a day's catch is worth, but naturally I always make a rough calculation.

Although at first glance many of the main merchants appear to be absent, the bidding is brisk and the catch is sold and at a very good price. Fred and I can rest in the knowledge that all our efforts have been well worth while as we walk back down the slipway and climb aboard the Dor-Bet, thinking that our day's work is more or less finished. How wrong can one be?

Fred has not forgotten the white motorboat with the blue wheelhouse, now just about visible some three or four miles off outside the harbour. "They are definitely in trouble!" Fred states in his loud abrupt way, leaving no room for argument. And the wind is freshening fast.

My thoughts are on the net that we tore rather badly and that has to be mended. We have now been on the move many hours without sleep and there is much to do before we put to sea again the following night. We have approximately twelve hours to get washed up, sleep, eat, and mend the net which is down to me. As a cockle fisherman, Fred has never learned to net.

Fred gets the binoculars out of the wheelhouse and concentrates on the speck in the distance for several seconds. She is still side to the wind and looks to be rolling heavily. If we don't do something soon, he almost shouts at me, we might be too late.

I resign myself to the fact that the day is far from over and start the Dor-Bet's engine. Once more we are running at full speed out into the Channel. Who said that a fisherman's life is an easy one? To make matters worse, the northerly wind was still freshening fast.

Steaming out to the little motorboat was a doddle. The now white-topped swell was directly astern. The wind had veered to the north even more and was now broad off the land, and the sun was shining brightly. In the harbour it had developed into a really beautiful day. But the further we progressed into the Channel the more it became obvious that the return journey was going to be most uncomfortable. The little boat had now drifted some six miles from the land. The closer we got the more she appeared to be in need of assistance. Side to the now quite vicious swell, she was rolling heavily. Two rather desperate figures were hanging on for dear life. Fred had been right to be concerned.

As we come closer to the distressed vessel Fred is sitting on the foredeck with a rope at the ready. We have decided that it will be wise to take the two occupants out of the boat first, then take her in tow if possible. That's if they agree. Then if the weather deteriorates too much we can always cast the boat adrift. Always there are far too many *ifs*.

We are now coming alongside and I can see that Fred's tongue is hanging out. He has a big grin on his face. I fail to see the funny side of the situation and concentrate on getting alongside without damaging either vessel, I tell Fred to have one of our double-rubber-tyre fenders ready. It's not going to be that easy to get the two crew members aboard without doing some damage.

The small, twenty-foot vessel looks quite fragile. It is at this moment that I see the reason for Fred's grin. One of the crew members is a young female dressed only in a bikini. She also looks quite fragile as she scrambles aboard the Dor-Bet. The young man who is her companion drops the rope (that Fred has thrown) over the little boat's bollard and makes a dive for his life. He is sick all over the deck of the Dor-Bet and looks in rather a sorry state. Fred takes a turn under the stern cleat and I say a silent thank-you as we take the boat in tow. It's going to be a hard pull back into Folkestone Harbour.

As I turn from the steering wheel with the intention of checking that all is going according to plan, I am clasped in a tight bear hug and soundly kissed on the lips by the young lady wearing the bikini. To say that I am somewhat taken aback is an understatement. This is the first female to set foot on the deck of the Dor-Bet and she is no ordinary female. She had no reserve or inhibitions whatsoever but plenty of everything else, and all of it in the right places. She introduces herself as Candy and as she speaks she turns and prods the young man (who is continuing to be sick) with her foot. "And this is Lord Edward! He does not look much like a lord at the moment," she states with a laugh. "It would appear that we are very much in your debt."

We are standing just inside the wheelhouse door and stopping Fred from coming in. It is quite obvious that he is enjoying the situation immensely and is about to lift the young lady out of his way, I quickly pull her inside the wheelhouse and out of his reach. Fred laughs out loud and offers her a nice cup of tea. She says she would love one.

Fred is really a very kind, thoughtful person, but his rough manner and size often tend to make people nervous when they first meet him. Not Candy. She appears to consider him rather cute. When he offers her my best spare jumper to put on, she also gives him a big kiss. Fred is over the moon and states that this could be one of our best trips yet, I don't think he is talking about the fishing.

The Dor-Bet is once more dipping her bows into the swell. Every time a solid wall of water hits the wheelhouse, Candy lets out a shriek of excitement. Poor Lord Edward is still lying out on the deck, getting very wet. Fred brings another cup of tea up out of the galley and tries to tempt him into eating some dry bread (good for seasickness) but he refuses the bread and tea and says he just wants to die. Candy is now standing at and holding the steering wheel. We now have a new skipper. A much better-looking one, according to Fred.

The return tow back into Folkestone Harbour took more than two hours. I was forced to reduce power for fear of swamping the little motorboat. She is very bluff-headed and not built to withstand the sort of conditions that exist in the English Channel with a northerly gale. We arrive thankfully without mishap and quickly moor to a barge which regularly lies alongside the outer pier. Hopefully we shall be able to remain here until we put to sea again later on this evening. It is now almost midday and there is much to do before that can happen.

We now know that Lord Edward and Candy are only staying in Folkestone on a long weekend break. Lord Edward, who has now somewhat recovered from his ordeal, is most anxious to get the little boat back onto its trailer and return to the hotel where they have been staying. Candy is not so keen, She has obviously enjoyed the adventure and is not too keen for it to come to an abrupt conclusion, but I insist that we have a great deal of work to do, and that we may possibly see them later. It is with some considerable relief on my part that Candy agrees to depart. She has a very disturbing influence on the Dor-Bets crew and the skipper. That's putting it mildly.

Fred and I discuss the question of claiming salvage. Fred is completely correct when he states that we have every right to do so. Claiming salvage can get very involved and complicated. I think we have as much on our plate as we can handle at the moment. Eventually Fred agrees.

Lord Edward insists on taking my address and telephone number before he left, insisting that he would be in contact some time in the future. Somehow I have my doubts.

Fred and I get washed and changed, and head across the harbour towards the Ark café. Most of the local boats have now landed and many of the fishermen go in for a cup of tea and a chat before going home. The Ark also provides a very large meal at a reasonable price. We had become friendly with the owners the previous year. Fred had really made a hit with Big Mabel, who served behind the counter and took all the orders. Fred is grinning and his tongue is hanging out; he is obviously looking forward to renewing the friendship. He has a certain, rough, special kind of charm that Big Mabel found totally disarming. I am looking forward to the confrontation.

Just like a gladiator entering the arena to do battle, Fred strode into the Ark café, marched up to the counter, and looking big Mabel straight in the eye, almost shouted, "Double eggs, double bacon, double pie, double sausages," and was about to say "double chips" at the very moment Big Mabel rammed a sausage in his mouth. Fred nearly choked. He swallowed hard and then said twice, "Please, Mabel."

The café is almost full of fishermen and holiday makers. Just for a split second there is complete silence as Fred lifts Mabel's hand and gives it a gentle kiss. Then everyone roars with laughter, especially the group of fishermen sitting at a very large table in the far corner of the café. Val Noakes beckons over and enquires, "Was it true you had to go back out and catch the last two fish, you greedy young beggar?"

As he was speaking he was making room for Fred and me to sit at the same table.

"Yes," I replied, "and we caught them both but we had a real big serious problem. One was far too big for either of us to handle.

Val gave a quiet chuckle. "Yes," he said. "I watched her walk round the harbour."

Fred came over to the table with two enormous plates piled high with food and for the next fifteen minutes we were much too busy filling our stomachs to carry on a conversation. It gave me just a few minutes' thinking time for what we had achieved in the last thirty-six hours. I came to a definite conclusion. One hell of a lot.

Although we were awake most of the twenty-four hours in every day it always seemed that when Fred and I were working together time never appeared to be in plentiful supply. We were always rushing on to try to achieve another task; there was always more to do. It was great to sit and talk and yarn with other fishermen. We have all got so many stories to tell. In the Ark there was an atmosphere of peace and comfort. The time went all too quickly. I had a torn net to mend and we must get some sleep. We have only another nine hours before we put out to sea again. It's time we were on the move. We hurry round the harbour, climb down the steps, and once more we are in a little world of our own. Fred goes down below and gets his head down. He is soon snoring peacefully. He did warn me not to sit in the sun mending for too long. It had become very warm in the sheltered harbour. The sun was roasting.

On our arrival back on board the Dor-Bet I was surprised and also rather annoyed to find that our prize from the rescue was still laid alongside. I also noticed for the first time that her name was Little Neptune. The first thought that came into my head was that if it had not been for the fact that Fred was always alert and on the lookout for anything unusual, Little Neptune might now be resting on the seabed in Davy Jones's locker. I am annoyed because there might be the possibility that legally, as the rescuers we might be held responsible for her safety until she is moved to another berth or taken out of the water altogether. Before I pull the net out and get settled into a comfortable position to start mending I call out. All is quiet, no sign of any life whatsoever. I settle down on top of the hatches with the net hooked up on my toes and commence netting. My hands move automatically across the meshes and soon I am lost in a world of dreams as to how I came to be fishing down-channel and not in the Thames estuary. At this moment the Thames seems a mighty long distance away.

Our first day's catch, which we had landed and put on the market earlier in the day, had been a very lucrative one. Had I been working for myself and not in a family concern the financial rewards would have amounted to at least two weeks' wages for Fred and myself, but the way my father had developed the business over many years all the proceeds of out joint efforts went into the communal pot. I was happy with this arrangement, but at times it did make for some very strange situations and my bringing the boat down-Channel to fish was one of them.

I am working my father's boat, the Dor-Bet. My older brother Peter is at present skipper of a vessel named the Paul David, which is owned by Peter and myself. The other three vessels, all much the same size, are owned by my other three older brothers, Norman, Bram, and Ray. Ray is the most senior member of the family (naturally, after Father). But we all work independently. Peter and I team up in the winter to carry out pelagic and pair-boat fishing generally. We are financial partners, and if that sounds a mess I am not surprised. Not many people would ever understand the setup, but it was to continue for many years into the future. For the moment I am stuck with it.

All the boats belonging to the family had carried out a reasonably successful spring sole fishery in the Thames. This was concentrated mainly in the upper reaches where the Dover soles come every year to spawn. We had then moved our efforts over onto the Kent side of the Thames estuary, moving further east onto the Whitstable flats and into the Queens Channel for the skate (ray) fishery, This had also been a most important fishery for many years and one which I always found very enjoyable and in most years quite successful. As we moved closer to the summer, my brother Peter and I transferred our pursuit of the skate back to the north side of the Thames and along the Barrow sands. It was here that we made one of the largest catches of skate ever in the Thames estuary.

Fishermen from ports in and around the Thames estuary had trawled the Barrow sands for many years. My father had often told the story of when some fifteen or twenty of the old Bawley Beam trawlers would sail down river as far as the east Barrow Edge lightship against a strong easterly wind just for the one low-water haul. If when they arrived in position ready to shoot the trawl away the wind dropped (as it was inclined to do when the ebb tide ceased to run), the boats had sailed more than thirty miles for nothing. Without engines there was little that they could do other than make their way home again with the flood tide.

I personally fished along the Barrow sands soon after leaving school and had many good hauls of skate over a period of ten years. My first experience as skipper was along the west end of the sands, with my father as mate. Two hauls yielded almost a hundred skate. There always appeared to be plenty of seals on the huge sand banks. The banks stretched for ten miles and are made up of two parts with a narrow navigable channel fit only for shallow-draughted vessels: through the middle. The only other ground "fish" that swim around the sands are shrimps. The sand is very hard but turns into a kind of quicksand once it is covered with just a few inches of water. There are several beds of cockles on the sands which we exploited in later years.

Returning to the year prior to my coming down-Channel: My brother Peter had been working on the west end of the sands and I had been alternating between the south side and the north side, but on the east end some six miles away. It had always intrigued me that even if I returned to the same area to trawl several times in the same week, the skate (usually a very nervous fish) would keep coming back to replace the fish that I had caught. There just had to be a piggy bank of skate replenishing the ground somewhere.

Early one fine summer morning after having made one good haul of eighty skate, I left Fred in charge of the wheelhouse and climbed the Dor-Bet's twenty-foot-high mast. From this elevated position I could see over the top of the huge sand bank and also for many miles around. I could also see a narrow strip of water stretching from the navigable channel all the way into the centre of the east Barrow sand. Tomorrow we would find out just how deep that strip of water was.

After my climbing the mast on that lovely summer's day, the Dor-Bet made two more hauls, finishing with a total of one hundred and thirty large skate, quite a reasonable day's work providing the market held its price. Every fish weighed between ten and twenty pounds. We would expect at least ten shillings for each individual fish.

We breasted up with the Paul David on the passage home. We often did this when the weather allowed. Steaming back to port alongside each other gave us the chance to talk and plan tactics. Also, if there was a lot of gutting or net-mending to do we could give each other a hand. We both carried ship-to-shore radio but we never discussed confidential matters over the air. We decided that the next day we would investigate that narrow strip of water that nestled in the middle of the eastern end of the Barrow sands.

When we arrived home that same day, Father informed us that the market for skate was a little on the slow side. It might be wise to concentrate our efforts on mixed species. This news we had to ponder overnight. Prospects for mixed fish in home waters at this time of year were, to say the least, quite poor. The following morning when we turned out, it looked like being another beautiful day and we decided that we would continue with our plan.

When we arrived at the point where we intended to sound our way into the navigable channel, we were a little early on the tide. We wanted to enter the low-way, as it was named, and turn to port. We also wanted the sand to be dried out on either side.

A sunken wreck on the south side of the area we were entering had almost caused a disaster for the Dor-Bet on another occasion. Only Fred's sharp eyes had saved us from running over the top of the wreck when it was just showing above the surface. In his hurry to warn me Fred tripped over a coil of rope and fell overboard. He managed to get back on board without hurting himself, but it could have been very nasty. In bad weather conditions one wrong move can lose a life. It happens all too often at sea. The high top of the Barrow sand was just beginning to show. We would have another hour and a half to wait before sounding our way into the gully. We must go in at just the right time. A cup of tea was next on the menu.

Today's tide is what fishermen call a dead tide. With just a slight breeze blowing from the northwest, it is not likely to be a very big ebb. The conditions should be ideal for our purpose.

We have decided to keep complete radio silence and this has not gone unnoticed. Other vessels from the surrounding ports have commented on the fact that we are not on the air. They assume that we must be up to some mischief or other. The exchanges are flowing thick and fast. They are all well aware that we have certain signals and code words that we use when we want to be incognito. For the moment we stay silent. This causes even more banter.

Peter heads for the south side of the gully and begins sounding, heading for what we know will eventually be a dead end. As the Paul David slowly noses her way in, Fred and I in the Dor-Bet carry out the same manoeuvre on the north side of the gully. The two boats are only some three hundred yards apart and we are both taking soundings with a twenty-foot-long pole that we keep especially for such an occasion as this. We ease our way into the narrow gully with great care. This is the first time ever that we have explored this particular strip of water and it is more than possible that stumps from an old wreck of some description may be sticking up from the seabed. We progress very slowly, our engines just ticking over.

Peter's mate, Belgie Joe, has hold of the pole and is doing the sounding on the Paul David. Fred is doing the same on the Dor-Bet.

Joe signals that he can feel cockles on the bottom. He thumps the pole into the ground several times to transmit this news to Fred, who then tells me and also confirms that the ground beneath us is still smooth sand, no sign of cockles.

The water beneath the two boats is slowly becoming more shallow but we still have two fathoms of water underneath the keel. We can keep going until there is only five feet. Fred keeps sounding and passing on information and I keep my eye fixed on the Paul David in case they run out of water.

Suddenly Joe appears to have gone crazy. He is jumping up and down, flapping his arms like a bird and at the same time pointing down into the water. And at that moment I know he is signalling that he can see skate swimming on the seabed.

I turned the Dor-Bet toward the south side of the gully and heading for a position approximately one hundred yards east of the Paul David. She was already turning and her trawl was going over the side in a great hurry. As we started to shoal the water up the steep into one and a half fathoms (just nine feet depth of water), Fred said he could feel the cockles on the bottom of the sounding pole. At the same instant we saw dark shapes gliding around on the seabed. It was not possible to know what numbers of skate were feeding on the cockle beds as the water had just a little colour in it. It was not "clear as gin." But there appeared to be a great many. I turned the Dor-Bet in a circle and we shot the trawl away. We were now towing the trawl along the bottom in the direction of the Paul David.

I had no idea what to expect. I was fully aware that we were experiencing an adventure of a nature that we had never even come close to before. The Paul David was now only some seventy yards ahead of us but we never even came close.

The trawl was on the sea-bed no more than six minutes when the otter doors started to come together, closing the net at the same time as the Dor-Bet came to a dead stop. The net was full of skate. Unbelievable.

We had fished only six minutes, but we worked for more than two hours getting the fish on board. It was impossible to count the exact numbers. Our estimation was in the region of three hundred and fifty. We made another, shorter haul, but even so caught a further three hundred. In just ten minutes of actual towing time we had a catch of six hundred and fifty skate.

We came alongside and breasted up with the Paul David. Her decks were also full to overflowing with skate. Between us we had made a catch of over thirteen hundred, large, mostly female skate. The decks were also littered with dozens of egg pouches, showing that the fish had recently shot their eggs.

We had obviously found the nursing home where the female skate came to recouperate after having laid their eggs.

We decided that we would have to give the gully a name. Belgie Joe suggested "The Hospital," and that's what it was christened. And the name was to stay forever.

As we headed back towards our home port of Southend-on-Sea there was much to think about. It was going to take many hours to get the skate winged and washed, ready for market. Our catch was by far the largest that we had ever made, and so far as we knew the most skate to be caught ever in one trip around our coast.

We had only been under way about thirty minutes when we were literally forced to heave to. A fishing vessel from Whitstable blocked our passage. As the skipper was a friend of many years (by the name of Alf Legget), we had to stop and speak. He took one look at the deep-loaded boats and shouted, "My God! I knew you young buggers were off the air for a reason. Where did you catch that lot! I have never seen so many skate at one time in my whole life."

Although we never liked to give away trade secrets, because he was such a good friend we gave him a rough indication of where we had been working, and informed him that he would have to hurry as the tide had started to flow and he could be too late. The TTFN steamed away to the east at full speed. We later learned that he did make a reasonably good catch.

Many hours later we had at last managed to get all the fish washed, boxed, and ready for the market. Father shook his head in disbelief when he first saw the enormous stack of boxes, full of skate wings. He had to smile but at the same time warned us that the market was poor. Father always insisted that a good fisherman worked according to the demands of the market. He warned us not to expect a very high price.

Such a huge landing of fish should have made close to a month's wages. The following morning we waited for the market prices to come over the phone before putting to sea. As Father had predicted, prices were far worse than poor. We were bitterly disappointed. The day's catch made less than half what we would have expected, even on a bad market. We would rather have left the fish swimming. With this nasty taste in my mouth, I decided to make a trip down-Channel in search of mixed fish as Father had requested. As Fred remarked, so far as the sale of fish was concerned, Father was usually right.

I have been sitting on the hatches of the fish hold with my back to the wheelhouse, lost in my dreams of the past. My mind clock tells me that almost three hours must have passed since I commenced to net. Fortunately the strength of both selvages down either side of the net had stopped the damage from being major. None of the net was missing. It was a straight mending-repair job.

Cutting into the selvages on either side made it possible for me to pick up the untorn meshes and mend in from both sides towards the bosom of the net, until the two came together. This I had completed. I now had to pick up a section of net that hung onto the cod-end and join this back up to the centre. The repair would then be complete.

I had been facing the stern all the time. In order to work from the cod-end up, I had to turn round the opposite way and face the wheelhouse. Another thirty or forty minutes would see the whole net back to normal. I turned and settled down once more, with the net hooked on my toes.

The part of the harbour that we were berthed in was commercial. There was very little activity at this moment and all was peace and quiet. In the whole time that I had been repairing the net I had hardly heard a sound. When I lifted my eyes in order to see the wheelhouse clock, I was astounded to find Candy (topless!), wearing just the bottom of her bikini, leaning contentedly with her back against the wheelhouse. I was speechless.

It was only now that I realized just how hot the sun had become. Earlier I had taken my shirt off and draped it over my head (for protection), tying the sleeves under my chin. I was bare-chested to the waist, and at the moment very disturbed. So disturbed that in my panic, I stabbed the quick of my thumb with the netting needle. And just to make matters worse: It drew blood. Quick as a flash Candy jumped to the rescue. Handkerchief at the ready, she grabbed my hand, at the same time draping herself over me. I was left helpless with the forbidden fruits from the garden of Eden hanging within biting distance just in front of my face, while she wiped the blood from my thumb. I was in pain, but the pain had nothing to do with the wounded thumb.

Unexpected help came from Fred. The sound of the kettle being filled and stood on the gas-range could be heard coming from the cabin. Fred was awake and would soon be on deck. Candy left just as silently as she had come, leaving me shell-shocked and more than a little light-headed. I was saved, but from what! The chances were I would never know.

Fred has made me a cup of tea and stands it on the hatch beside me. He arrives just as I make the last knot and cut the netting needle free of the net. He then proceeds to give me a good scalding. In his loud, threatening voice, he says, "Your determination will be the death of you before long." There is no answer to this. I am well aware that I am very tired and have worked in the heat of the sun for much longer than was good for me.

I notice that Fred is sniffing the air and glancing over at the Little Neptune, still laid alongside. I keep imagining I can smell that girl's perfume! He shouts, giving his big toothy grin. She was quite something. I give a grunt of agreement and drink my tea in silence, wondering at the same time if she might be listening on board the Little Neptune. We usually go ashore for a drink in the evening, but I must get some rest. Fred decides to go alone. I go down below and turn in.

We have cushions on the lockers. When the weather is warm enough, we just strip down to our underpants and lie on the locker. The Dor-Bet's tiny cabin is inclined to be rather stuffy. The only air coming in is via the hatch that opens into the wheelhouse. One way in and the same way out. The two lights are on the front of the engine-room bulkhead and are sufficient for our needs. Turning off the lights, I close my eyes and try to sleep. I know that sleep is going to be difficult! I am past the point of natural sleep. It will more than likely be four hours of restless dreams. Then it will be time to put to sea once more. Gradually I drift away.

Some considerable time must have elapsed before reality tried to creep into my dreams. My mind was sometimes on the torn net. Then Val Noakes was telling me we should have claimed salvage. We had every right.

Then I could see my brother Peter's mate (Belgie Joe) sounding the depth of water with a long pole. Joe had died at sea on board the Paul David after having suffered a heart attack, not long after we landed the enormous haul of skate. That was now more than two years past. My mind is going round and round in circles.

Then someone lands on the deck with a loud thud, but it's all in my dreams. I am no longer alone in the cabin. This is not in my dreams.

In my completely confused state of mind I am telling myself that Fred cannot be in two places at once. As if from a great distance I can hear his voice, in no uncertain terms telling somebody that the boat will have to be moved when we put to sea in about an hour's time. If Fred is up in the harbour, who is trying to incite me to run riot? A pair of hands is giving me a complete once-over. Without question I am now wide awake.

At the first sound of voices coming from up top, the attack on my body ceases. There is the sound of a body of some kind making a very hasty retreat.

For several seconds I lie still, not really prepared to accept the reality of what has just taken place. In my vivid imagination I can see the newspaper headlines: Skipper attacked in fishing boat's cabin. In the half-light of the cabin I start to laugh at my predicament until Fred's loud voice shouts, "What the devil are you laughing at? You won't think its so funny if we miss the dark fishing—and I can still smell that girl's perfume!"

Fred makes a cup of tea while I check the engine and prepare the Dor-Bet for a rapid departure. If we lose even one hour of the dusk or dark fishing, the end result could be the loss of half a night's work. Within ten minutes we are steaming full speed out of the harbour. I am praying that we shall have a quiet, untroubled night.

As we shoot the trawl away for the first time this trip, and settle down for a three-hour tow, I once again count my blessings and realize just how fortunate a person I am. The moon is full and shining bright. Millions of stars glitter in the heavens, And the block-ship has just become visible some two miles ahead. Fred once again clears the deck, ready for when we make our first haul, then sets about cooking the one-legged crab. Supper is going to be crab rolls with plenty of salt and pepper, with a side dish of tomatoes to suck at the same time. Let's hope the wind doesn't freshen in the night. It could stir things up somewhat.

Tonight we are going to have plenty of company. There are very few secrets on an open market and word has gone round that we had made a good catch the previous night. The Folkestone boats are out in full force. It looks like it might be an exciting experience. There is always something new, never a dull moment, and I have already forgotten that I have had only three hours sleep in the last two days.

My life in general has been what most normal people would consider totally chaotic. The last forty-eight hours have been no exception. Even so, I had managed to find those few essential moments that had allowed me to map out plans for the day's fishing.

It's no surprise that we have the company of some of the Folkestone boats, but I had not expected the whole fleet. I would need to change part of my plan accordingly.

It is common knowledge that fishermen who carry out most of their operations in the deep waters of the oceans dislike working in the shallows. The Folkestone men are no exception. As La-La has said to me on several occasions, "We don't like the bloody braces," meaning the towing wire, "up round our bloody necks."

Having cut my teeth in the shallow waters of the Thames estuary, I make these working conditions my natural habitat. Rather than make life too complicated by getting in the way of the slightly bigger local vessels, we will complete the first haul after three hours, then move inside the block-ship, even closer to the land and in as little as six feet of water.

As usual, Fred has brought the crab and butter rolls from the cabin up into the wheelhouse. This is a time when we get a few minutes to chat about old times, also what has taken place recently, and what might happen during the next twenty-four hours.

Fred was still concerned about Lord Edward and Little Neptune. He had spoken to Lord Edward just before we had put to sea. It had been Fred's loud voice ordering him to move the Little Neptune from alongside that had roused me from my dreams. In Fred's opinion we would have been much better to have made a complete job of the rescue and claimed salvage. He also made the point that Candy—whom he considered to be downright dangerous—would return. I decided it would be wise to keep quiet. We munched away contentedly on our crab rolls and sucked our juicy tomatoes. At least Candy could not interfere with with us while we were out at sea. For the next twenty-four hours, we were reasonably safe. Fred went out on deck to prepare for when the fish would be coming aboard. I started to plan our movements for the time when we had made the first haul and would be moving in closer to the land. We were fishing on excellent ground. But as is usually the case, there were one or two obstacles.

The first haul of the night swung on board with a loud thump as it came into contact with the restraining hatch. The cod-end bag was not quite as large as the first dark haul on the previous night, but proved to be more valuable. The soles were far better quality and there were three large turbot. Twelve stone of good marketable soles plus the three turbot. Already we had a reasonable night's work just in the first haul. It never ceased to amaze me how easy it could be, yet sometimes so damned hard. There had been many times in my fishing life when, as it says in the Bible, the fishermen toiled all night and caught nothing. It had not happened that many times—but it had happened. Here we were on a beautiful summer's night, having been at sea only some four hours, and we had a good night's work. The quality of this first haul of the night would sell them on almost any market.

Having made such a good start to the night's fishing now gave me confidence to perhaps trespass onto dangerous ground.

The local vessels now surrounded us completely. It was time to make a move and get out of their way.

Some four miles east of the block-ship there was a military gunnery-practice range. The previous year I had received an official warning to keep out or the boat would be impounded and what's more, I would be arrested. This caused me a problem, as the area it covers is excellent sole ground. I tell Fred we are going inside the block-ship and shoot away to the east towards Folkestone. I can almost read the questions in his mind; he only grunts.

Always when we are trawling in the night I leave the gutting to Fred. Far too many things can go wrong if one loses concentration. The cleaning and boxing of the fish can wait until daylight if need be. Its far more important that we stay clear of trouble.

In the process of reaching the gunnery range, we will have to pass two underwater obstructions which I have come fast on before. I believe one is a bomber plane shot down in the second world war, and the other just a load of old stumps, possibly an old boat that has almost disappeared into the ground but capable of tearing the net to smithereens. It is my intention to tow past these obstructions, keeping in close to the land and leaving them on our starboard side. I have achieved this successfully before.

Last year whilst towing past one of the wrecks, the Dor-Bet had slowly come to a standstill. At the time I thought that maybe we had filled the net with weed. We had recovered a small set of trawl gear that had been lost by one of the tiny boats that land on the beach at Hythe. We had returned the net and gear at the first opportunity and made a friend for life. It's strange how all these little adventures go towards making a fisherman's life so different and so interesting.

Although I had carried out this haul on one other previous occasion, I was taking no chances. It was not possible to take visual marks of the land or determine our position with the echo sounder or depths of water. There had been numerous bumps on the seabed: on the land side and on the seaward side of the two obstructions. This could easily have changed since we were here last year. The land appeared to be very close, standing out starkly in the darkness that had descended after the moon had gone down. Distances on the sea could be very deceptive. It was impossible to calculate accurately the exact distance between the Dor-Bet and the land. I was navigating purely on instinct.

As has happened so many times in my life when I have been taking risks, help came from an unexpected direction in the actions of another vessel, in fact two other vessels. One of the larger Folkestone ships had decided to keep us company in the shoal water. This was a bit risky—to say the least!—as he would need seven or eight feet of water just to stay afloat.

Not being absolutely certain (in the dark) which ship it was, I just waited to see what movements he intended to carry out and also in which direction the skipper was going to tow the trawl. I turned on my radio and switched to the trawler band, something the Folkestone vessels hardly ever bothered to do. It was for this reason that my radio was switched off. Also in the night it became unbearably noisy because of the amount of static interference. The engine noise (directly under my feet) was more than enough. I preferred the peace and quiet.

The unknown vessel was approximately three parts of a mile east of our position. As far as I could ascertain, if she towed to the west in our direction she would pass on our seaward side, and quite close at that. Almost within shouting distance.

The moment I was certain that he had shot his trawl and settled down, I called on the radio. *Vessel towing to the west of the target area in the bay. Do you receive me?* Complete silence, apart from the static. I called again several times. No answer.

If my calculations were correct, the vessel was towing somewhere in the line of the sunken boat, one of the obstacles I was trying to keep clear of. Both vessels were converging on the wreck and coming towards each other fast. We would not be long finding out. I was reluctant to try closing the land any further. We were close enough.

There was a scream of brakes as winch drums ran out and the other vessel stopped. Fred had gone forward to sit on the Samson post where it was less noisy. He came back to tell me that there was plenty of shouting; in fact, the air was blue. It sounded as if La-La was fluffing again! I had tried my best to warn him. We found out much later that they removed several bulks of timber from the old wreck.

The larger ship that berthed at Folkestone and was fast on the wreck was more than capable of taking care of herself. They always carried at least three in the crew, and were well equipted to deal with almost any problems that they encountered. If the vessel had been smaller than the Dor-Bet, we would have hauled the net and offered assistance. With all these thoughts running through my mind, we continued towing towards the gunnery ranges, which were now some two miles ahead.

A mental picture of what had taken place in the last ten minutes flashed across my mind. During the time that the other vessel had been coming towards us, I remembered just for an instant catching sight of another, smaller combination of navigation lights, three or four miles to the east and well outside of the ranges but steaming head-first in our direction and also towards the land. This had slipped from my mind at the time but came back to me now as I weighed up our situation. Visibility was good (even if it was dark) but the other small vessel had vanished from the scene. I warned Fred to keep a sharp look-out.

We had now been towing on this haul for about an hour. If it was possible, I wanted to continue towing in an easterly direction until daylight, which was about two hours away. This would take us into the ranges and out on the other side. I was taking a gamble that providing the ground had remained undisturbed all night, the risk would be well worth taking. The fishing should be good.

Fred remained for'ard on the lookout. My greatest fear at this moment was that the vessel that had vanished had darkened ship and moved onto the prohibited area before us. We had approximately one mile to tow, then we too would darken ship. It would be asking for trouble to enter the gunnery range with lights blazing. Then, it was asking for trouble to enter under any circumstances.

With a slightly disturbed mind and keeping very alert I went ahead with my plan. The restful night that I had hoped for was about to be shattered. Big Time.

The first indication of anything out of the ordinary was a single dim white light heading towards us. Fred tapped on the wheelhouse window and came aft to warn me. We were still very close to the land.

I could recollect on one other occasion seeing a similar light at the masthead of a cobble that had launched from the beach (just west of Hythe), but the light was not bright enough. Fred came aft once again and putting his head in the wheelhouse, shouted, "It looks as though this boat has a torch as a masthead light." He went back for'ard and sat on the Samson post once more.

It entered my mind that I might try to squeeze between this light and the land. But I lacked the courage. My gut feeling said I was already treading dangerously. I gently eased the Dor-Bet to starboard, allowing passage for the light to go inside of us.

Tensed and ready for the unexpected as I was, my heart almost stopped beating when Fred slammed his fist against the side of the wheelhouse as he raced aft. His head came into the glare of the deck lights. His tongue was hanging out but he wasn't grinning. ("It's a bloody watchman on a bike," he shouted.) I swung the wheel hard-over and sheared away from the land, not daring to breathe.

We both sat in silence for several minutes, giving ourselves time to recover from the shock. Little did we know that the night was far from over. I warned Fred about the other small boat that had seemingly vanished into thin air (or water). He went reluctantly back up for'ard and sat on the Samson post once more. It was turning into quite a night. We were entering the gunnery ranges. (I darkened ship.)

We were now both on red alert. I had warned Fred that the slightest noise or movement I wanted to know about. His reply came back with more than a little sarcasm. If anything else happened, he was going home. His tongue wasn't hanging out. Neither was he grinning.

Fred barely had time to settle down on his lookout post. We had only moved into the ranges ten minutes' towing time, when it appeared all hell was let loose! A stream of red tracer shells raced across the Dor-Bet's bows, no more than the length of two cricket pitches ahead and less than forty feet above the line of our twenty foot-high mast. It was as if we had entered a war zone. Our night was totally shattered.

I was already turning the Dor-Bet round with the intention of getting out of the ranges pronto. The surprises had not yet finished. Lots of lights had now been turned on! Only just ahead of where we had previously been towing, a vessel was hauling its gear in great haste. What's more, I recognized that display of deck lights. We had been joined in battle by brother Peter and he was certainly receiving a warm welcome.

I decided not to try to make contact with brother Peter until after break of day. The less anyone knew about our being there together, the better it would be. We had towed into the range area with darkened ship. It was just possible that our presence had not been noticed. We kept towing back west towards the block-ship unit daybreak. I was very careful not to get in anyone's way. When the day had brightened enough to haul the gear without lights, we did so.

We were rewarded with one of the best hauls I ever made down-Channel. Such a mixture of large soles and enormous plaice of top quality, the like of which I had never seen before. There were also seven lobsters, almost a box of crabs, four turbot, and two more brill. There were even a dozen John Dorys. It was a bumper haul with hardly any discard what-so-ever.

We moved much further off into the eleven-and-twelve fathom line! Now that it was fully daylight, what little draft of wind existed was from a northwesterly direction, leaving the water clear as gin. It was time to chase the plaice and dogfish once more. We shot the gear away in twelve fathoms paying out the towing wires until we had a blue fifty-fathom mark on the stern. Only then did I switch the radio on, just in case brother Peter called.

Fred came into the wheelhouse, sat down on his seat opposite me, and gave a huge toothy grin, then burst into loud laughter. "How could you describe that night to anyone!" he said, shaking his head. "If I had not been here with you, even knowing the sort of scrapes you get yourself into, I would never have believed it. Just magic…"

Fred went down to the cabin with the intention of making a bacon sandwich and a cup of tea. I relaxed on my seat in the wheelhouse, keeping one eye on the echo-sounder. The day was gradually developing into a scorcher. Every twenty minutes or so I went outside on deck and dipped my head into a bucket of water, just to make sure that I didn't nod off. Sleep was a commodity which I was not managing to get much of. I looked down into the cabin with the intention of asking Fred where my tea had got to. It must have been a very demanding night; Fred had fallen asleep on the job! First time ever.

All day I nursed the thought that two lorry loads of troops might be waiting on the harbour when we landed. With this in mind I had decided to fish on through the whole day. For the time being I would let Fred sleep on, possibly for a couple of hours or more. We could catch up with gutting and washing later. It would also give Peter the chance to make up a day's work.

The one way we might lose out by doing this is that we would be landing on the last of the tide. Also on the last of the market, which could make an enormous difference to the value of our catch.

It was most important that we kept clear of the military. Our name was not quite so well known in this part of the world and we could be in big trouble. My radio was still switched on. Peter had not attempted to call, or anybody else for that matter.

Fishing down-Channel was so totally different from working in the Thames estuary. With five family boats working together and more often than not combining their efforts similar to a fleet of mine-sweepers, it was often difficult to command any air space at all. There were also lots of other small boats in the area. Most carried radios, making the trawler band very busy. Added to this (when conditions were favourable), we also received the occasional Scotsman (working the herrings) and singing gospel songs at the same time. It was a right mixture, to say the least.

When our five family boats all arrived on the Whitstable flats at the same time, it usually produced quite a bit of ribbing on both sides, and sometimes got a little bit out of hand. But most of the time the remarks were given and received in the right spirit. We never knew when we might need each other's help. It was not wise to forget this fact. The sea could quite often be a very dangerous place without the presence of a few friends.

From the position at the steering wheel where I was sitting Fred was not in my line of vision. I was forced to lean over towards the centre of the wheelhouse in order to see down into the cabin. I reached round the half bulkhead, found the switch on the back of the bulkhead, and turned the lights on. Fred was still snoring. I decided to let him dream on for another hour.

2

My mind (once again) began to wander back over the years before Fred had first joined me and become my right-hand man. I marvelled at the speed of change since the end of the second world war, especially in the methods of fishing.

I had served my apprenticeship at many of the old-fashioned ways catching, which would now be considered a joke. Fred had joined me just before one of the last methods was discontinued.

At the age of eleven I was going to sea at regular intervals, in fact every time the tides were right and I was not compelled to attend school.

There was an abundance of fish. It was not necessary to go miles out to sea, the fish were on the doorstep, literally…

My father was using fishing methods that had been around for many years. Some, hundreds of years. One of these methods was long-lining. I made my first voyage when I had just passed my eleventh birthday.

We first had to walk off on the mud alongside Southend Pier (which extended for more than one and a half miles into the estuary), dig the mud for log-worm, and then bait two thousand hooks. When this was all completed, the lines were transported off outside Southend Pier (in Father's eighteen-foot-long skiff) and shot in an area known as the Middle Ground. The lines were laid at one low-water, then hauled on the next.

Each time one set of lines was hauled, they were replaced with a second set. That's if the weather was fit. We were in the middle of a cold-hard winter.

My first voyage was so exciting that despite the cold my whole body was tingling with the rush of blood through my veins. We caught almost a hundred large cod, all weighing between eight and fourteen pounds.

My father was also using an old type of beam trawl for catching shrimps when they were in season.

One of the most successful and quite important fisheries in spring and summer was the Peter-net fishing. This stop-net method of catching fish dated back hundreds of years in one form or another. These nets were mainly used for catching skate. They also proved to be very efficient when used for catching plaice (on Boxing Day, just six weeks after my first experience with the cod).

My father informed that he was going to try the Peter nets for plaice on the fore-shore below Southend Pier. So far as he knew, this had not been tried before. Several plaice had been seen swimming in one of the guts at a time when the tide was out. He thought it would be worth a try.

Each Peter net was fifteen fathoms long and two fathoms deep; twelve nets for each eighteen-foot skiff (in three sets of four), needing fifteen anchors to keep them in place on the seabed.

It was six A.M. on a fine Boxing Day morning when we shot the nets over the stern of the old skiff (named Curlew) and two hours later when we hauled.

This day was one of the rare occasions when my Father displayed great excitement;. His exact words were, "Loll, You must be a lucky charm." We had caught one hundred and twenty stone of plaice. Not large fish, but large enough for market. It was a nice Christmas box.

The small skiff was fully loaded, leaving her with only six inches of free-board. It was very fortunate that the old Curlew was now resting on the sand. The tide had ebbed and for the next two hours she would be high and dry. She could be made shipshape and land on the first of the flood-tide.

Fred had come to work with me on the Dor-Bet at a time when all of these old methods of catching fish were coming gradually to an end. I had by this time become the appointed Peter-net fisherman of the family. I suppose I was the most experienced.

In the very early days (when I first left school), one of the most interesting parts of my apprenticeship was learning the names of all the different areas of ground that we were working at that time, and also the many compass courses needed to reach these grounds. I had been out of school three years before the opportunity came to examine a chart of the Thames estuary. Everything was learned the hard way.

I could recite the names of all the many guts, Swins, high-tops, and dreans from Southend-On- Sea going east all the way to the black water some forty miles down the estuary, and there were quite a few. I say "were" because they change from one year to the next. Most years, hundreds of millions of tons of sand move. The contours of the seabed are forever changing.

We had been catching sea-moss (white weed). It had become a large and rather lucrative industry with more than forty vessels involved but was inclined to become rather boring. I decided it would make quite a nice change (and a good experience for Fred) if we went Peter-net fishing. I also thought the time and conditions were right for making a reasonable catch. At the time of my leaving school there had been eight Peter-net boats fishing the Maplin sands outside Foulness. At this point of time just one remaining family worked the grounds on a regular basis. They were Guy and Harry Wilkinson.

We had to get all the nets and anchors out of our net store and into the skiff on the previous day. It involved a considerable amount of work. I did begin to wonder if it was worth all the effort. In order to make the trip we had to turn out one hour before high water—five A.M on the dot. No question of arriving late.

The next day as we prepared to go on board and get under way, we encountered a slight problem. The sun came up and it shut in thick fog. This was not a very good start to what I was hoping would be a nice relaxing day, but we could cope with the fog. I was determined that one way or another we were going Peter-net fishing. There was a good chance the fog would clear once the sun got a proper hold. We would continue with our plan and with a little bit of luck, all would be well.

All of the family vessels had put in a full week at the whiteweed fishery, long, hard days from first light throughout the long hot summer's day until night stopped operations. Dredging the weed off the seabed was a very arduous task which demanded much effort and persistence. The sea seldom gave up its great wealth easily. Catching and cleaning the sea-moss was no exception.

When this industry had first developed, we had not reached the point in time of installing winches in our small vessels. The four six-foot-wide dredges were pulled up from the seabed and manipulated ("Handrolickly" was the favourite word). It was not surprising that we all developed muscles almost as big as footballs. With the coming of belt-driven winches this had all changed. Nevertheless, it was still the type of work that sapped and drained the energy. It also lacked the excitement of trawling for fish. Taking the dense fog into the equation, I very much doubted that my brothers would make a move today. It was the last day of a very lucrative week.

The coming of the sea-moss boom had given our family business a tremendous financial lift, contributing in a big way to the success we were to enjoy throughout our lives.

All these thoughts ran through my mind in just the few minutes it took Fred and me to motor off to the Dor-Bet's mooring. We bumped alongside (on the fenders) with the skiff and stopped the small boat's engine. Visibility was less than twenty yards.

The Wilkinsons' boat was a Bawley, a very smart little ship named the Bona, moored only fifteen yards in-shore from the Dor-Bet where Fred and I were now preparing to get under way. I was just about to go into the wheelhouse and start the engine when they came off alongside in their own skiff.

Guy and Harry Wilkinson had been Peter-net fishermen all their lives. Guy was always the spokesman, also considered to be just about the most successful Peter-net fisherman ever. Much of what I had learned through the years about this type of fishing came from studying his methods. I had great respect for his skills. They had come for a chat.

Guy's first words were "I don't think it's going to clear today. We'll give it best and hope it clears for the morning. With the fog as thick as this we won't stand much chance of finding the right spot to shoot the nets. We are not quite as efficient as you without an echo sounder."

I was most surprised to hear Guy make this statement. The Wilkinsons had always been proud of their reputation. With tongue in cheek I invited them to join us and leave the Bona on her mooring. Much to my surprise, they accepted.

Fred cast off the mooring. I set a course in an easterly direction with the intention of passing through a gap in the old boom defence that still remained as a constant reminder that the dark days of the war were not that far back in the past. My course should bring us just north of the gap. We would then creep along the boom and find the gap, with a bit of luck.

It was quite early on the tide. We had no need to hurry and I suggested that we would prepare the nets for shooting once we arrived on the ground (in two hours' time). Guy agreed.

Fred was on his perch up for'ard on the Samson post, keeping a lookout for the boom. There was no sign of the fog's clearing. We carried a slow ebb tide from astern, pushing us toward the boom. Fred needed to keep his eyes peeled. The moment his hand came up to signal that he had sighted the boom I put the wheel hard over, bringing the Dor-Bet round on a southwesterly course. At the same time the boom became visible to me, allowing us to run parallel with it. I had my fingers crossed, hoping that my calculations had brought us to the right spot.

Just a few seconds later we spotted the gap in the boom defence, I swung the Dor-Bet back onto an easterly course and we passed safely through. We had cleared the first hurdle.

Switching on the echo sounder and noting the time, I increased the engine revs. The Dor-Bet was now pushing through the water at her normal motoring speed, with two skiffs astern. Providing we keep the correct courses and change course at the correct times, there are no further obstructions between us and the ground we are going to fish. Guy and Harry observe and keep silent. I say a little prayer. I am once more pushing my luck.

Our first target to be noted is when we begin to deepen the water into the Backtale gut. I point this out to Guy. He nods his head and remains silent. We shoal the water up onto the hightop below the Blacktale, then in just a few more minutes start to deepen the water once more, taking us into the clementina. Once again I notice Guy nod his head. We press on. Jordens, the Maplin flats into Kirby's, back of the sheers, into the tender trap.

I notice Guy smiles. He had given the tender trap its name. We press on into stump gut. Then into Lens drean, which is our destination. The drean is in two parts at this point in time. We shoal the water in the middle, then deepen once more into the main part. This has been excellent fishing ground in the past, yielding thousands of top-quality skate over the years. There is room enough for thirty Peter-nets in the main stream.

All the depths of water on the echo sounder look correct; the contours of the ground, just about right. We shoal the water on the hoss (which is the high-top on the lower side of the drean). I swing the Dor-Bet half-circle back in the direction we have just come. Deepen the water again and Fred is all ready to let go the anchor. We have arrived, I hope. Guy smiles and says, "bloody magic…"

At last the fog was beginning to lift! The sun had broken through, making our tasks much less difficult.

As Fred is new to the Peter-net fishing, Guy agrees that Arthur Plappet (their third hand) will help me lay the nets on the skiff's stern, ready for shooting over the stern. This will take the best part of an hour and we shall be using both skiffs for the job. This arrangement causes me no problems whatsoever as Arthur and I went to school together. We have always been good friends and get along just fine. Fred makes everyone a cup of tea. At the allotted time of three hours ebb (half ebb), the nets are all ready to go overboard.

As the nets have to be rowed out, I will do the rowing while Guy and Harry organise the shooting of the nets and anchors. All the nets will be shot in one straight line. They will take approximately fifteen minutes to go overboard and will be in the water actually fishing for just over two hours. In that time we eat and relax.

The time quickly passes. We have eaten bacon sandwiches and swapped stories about the old days, and when we have finished our tea we will leave the Dor-Bet and prepare to haul the nets. We are hoping that the nets will have remained nice and clean (no mucky weed or jellyfish) and with enough skate to make the day interesting and also worthwhile. We shall soon know.

The tide has ebbed quite quickly, leaving the nets in about three feet of water. We are motoring along the whole length of twenty-four nets. Fred is up on his toes, grinning. As usual his tongue is hanging out with excitement. We can see the ripples of many skate waking in the nets. The prospects look very promising.

From the time we started hauling the nets through to the finish took almost an hour. Both skiffs are fully loaded and we have caught almost five hundred skate and twenty-four large dogfish, all of them over six feet long. It has turned into a very successful day.

Fred and Arthur quickly became friends and settled into a good working relationship, which was just as well. A few short months later Peter's mate (Belgie Joe) died at sea of a heart attack on board the Paul David. Arthur became brother Peter's full-time mate and remained so for quite a number of years. Fred and Arthur would be working very close together whenever brother Peter and I paired up for the sprat and herring fishing in the winter. We were all to share many adventures together.

The sound of water going into the kettle quickly brought me back to the present time. Fred had obviously come back into the land of the living. He had been asleep just over two hours! It was very important that Fred get enough rest to take him through the day. Most of the night's catch stood on the deck in boxes, waiting to be gutted and washed. Hopefully, after we have hauled again there should be a great deal more. It was bad policy to get behind with cleaning of the fish. The quicker they were washed and boxed ready for market the better.

Sometimes it was possible to trawl and catch the fish, gut, and wash in a set routine that gave the impression that life as a fisherman was a piece of cake, and it could be just that simple. It was a totally different situation when working on soft mucky ground that compelled us to haul the trawl every twenty minutes. We could finish the day with a deck full of ungutted fish, three trawls to repair, and both Fred and I completely shattered after just a short eight-hour day. It had happened on many occasions since Fred had first come to sea with me on board the Dor-Bet.

I had been warned many times by well-meaning skippers that the English Channel was a terrible area of ground to work a trawl. I had found just the opposite. Compared with the Thames estuary, it was a doddle. My family had grown up with problems like green weed, cockle dirt, white weed and sack weed, sometimes making it necessary to haul the net every ten minutes. There was nothing to compare with this when working in the Channel. On the whole, it was very clean.

There is no doubt in my mind whatsoever that the most dangerous problems in the Thames estuary come from the amount of shipping traffic always present and a continuous threat to a fishing boat of any size. Many of the most prolific and best-yielding hauls actually crossed over the main shipping lanes. A vessel could be carrying all the correct signals in day or night fishing; a ship will seldom give any ground in the confined spaces that they have to deal with in the Thames estuary. They would rather run down a small fishing vessel than run the risk of losing their ship—which I suppose is only natural. Even in the time Fred has been my mate, I have had more near misses than I care to recall where only drastic action on my part prevented a complete disaster. I think one could truthfully say that trawling in the Thames estuary was, is, and always will be a dangerous way to earn a living.

It's turned into a really beautiful day with good visibility. Looking back astern across the bay towards Folkestone, I can see three small boats and I assume one of these boats is Brother Peter's. My radio has been switched on from the moment that I suspected that he and his mate Arthur had arrived (in the Paul David) to join us. He was obviously keeping radio silence after the shock of coming under fire during the night. I was not unduly concerned as we were bound to meet up with him sometime later in the day. At last Fred has arrived in the wheelhouse with tea and toast; I'm feeling a bit peckish, to say the least. We munch contentedly on the toast and discuss the day ahead. We shall be hauling again in twenty minutes. From that moment until the end of the day, Fred is going to have his work cut out keeping pace with all the gutting and washing. He has all the night's catch to clear and more (we hope) to come when we haul in in just a few minutes. It has all the signs of being a very busy day.

We have hauled the net and shot away again, and continue to tow in the direction of Dungeness point. As the nature of the ground changes, so does the catch.

This for me is possibly the most interesting difference in working the Channel. Our last haul has produced a variety of different species which we seldom if ever see on our home ground in the Thames. Spotted dogs, John Dorys, several lobsters and crabs, two five-pound octopuses, and several skate, another turbot, and three boxes of mixed plaice and sand dabs—what we in the fishing Industry would refer to as a right good mixture. All of these different types of fish add up to a bigger return in the market at the end of a trip.

Looking out of the wheelhouse door (once we have settled down again) I tell Fred that in just a few minutes I will be out on deck to give him a hand, He tells me he can manage. It will be another three hours before we make another haul. It is possible to make these extra-long hauls only because there is so little discard. Almost everything that comes on board in the net goes into the boxes. There is very little waste.

Watching Fred at work on the deck (cleaning, gutting, and separating the fish) reminds me how far he has come since the days when he raked cockles from the mud at Leigh-on-Sea. He is not yet the fastest person with a knife, but considering he was a late starter, neither is he slow. Meticulous in the routines, he has developed into a first-class hand over the time he has been working with me.

He has also had many unusual and exciting experiences: The enormous catch of skate in the gut on the Barrow sands which we named the Hospital; Peter-net fishing on the Maplin sands at the time when we took the Wilkinsons in tow; plus several further trips afterwards. The exciting spring fishery; trawling for skate on the Whitstable flats and the serious competition between the different boats involved and even the different ports. It was always very competitive.

Fred had also seen the Dor-Bet deep-loaded with sprats on more than one occasion. Not long after Fred first came with me, we had entered into our usual pair trawling for sprats with a mid-water pelagic trawl. This method of catching sprats developed just after the war, so different from the old fashioned stow-boaters (as the Bawley boats were called) who just followed the lines of birds as they fed on the fish and relied on the tide to bring the fish into the net after the Bawley had anchored. It was called standing against the tide. Very hit or miss. It was the arrival of echo sounders that enabled us to actually see the fish and at what depth they were swimming. This made the pelagic trawl so efficient and effective. We could not only see the fish, we were now able to follow the pattern of their movements.

We put to sea early one morning and at the beginning of the season. We had been working the hard-running tides and catching something like a ton of sprats in three or four hours' towing time. This was not considered very good. We had a debate, as so often happened. We decided to split our fishing effort in half, with two boats going further down the estuary into what we called the iron-bite. The other two would lie at Southend pier waiting for daylight, just in case the shoals of sprats came together on the low water.

Brother Norman in the Will-Glyn, myself in the Dor-bet; we thought the fish had already arrived in large numbers, they just hadn't gotten together because of the hard-running tide. We would wait at the pier for daybreak and the low-water time.

Brother Peter in the Paul-David and Brother Ray in the John Patrick would go further to sea. This was a combination of the boats which very seldom happened. Brother Peter and I almost always worked together. We lay alongside the pier. We had almost four hours to wait.

It was two hour's after high water when the four vessels cast off their moorings and headed out into the darkness (two hours' ebb). Brother Ray and Brother Peter heading for the open sea, Brother Norman and myself heading for the end of the pier, where we would wait until just before low-water. This would also be daybreak.

Brother Norman in the Will-Glyn went straight to the pier and berthed alongside. I wanted to have a look outside the pier and up towards the Low-way buoy. Was there going to be any quantity of fish at daybreak? I was expecting some signs of life on the echo sounder, perhaps two or three fathoms of hazy dots. This would give me some encouragement to believe that the sprats would be in the area somewhere at low-water (daybreak).

As we rounded the end of the pier and headed west, Fred was sitting next to me in the wheelhouse. He had so far not made any comment as to the plans that we had made; he was unusually quiet. He went down below to make a cup of tea. We could relax and enjoy that relaxation. We had nothing to do but wait.

We motored up to the west for about three hundred yards, shearing from one side of the deeper water to the other. There appeared to be just a light spattering of marks on the north side. I was satisfied with this. We returned to the pier and moored alongside the Will-Glyn. I joined Fred (down below in the cabin). We sat in silence, contentedly eating toast and drinking our tea. Fred posed a question.

He could not understand what we were doing differently from what we had been doing over the last two days. He thought I would have been more venturesome and headed out further to sea with Brother Peter. He made the point that this was the first time I had taken the easy way out since he had joined me some months before. It was totally out of character. I did not try to explain! He would just have to wait and see.

Fred lay back on the bunk and closed his eyes. "I might as well get some sleep even if it does look like it's going to be a quiet day. We don't appear to get one that often. It will make a nice change and I shall make the most of it."

One hour later I let go of the berthing ropes and carried out exactly the same exercise: rounded the end of the pier and headed up to the west for the second time that morning. I was encouraged at the change that had taken place in the time we had lain alongside the pier. The spattering of marks had now become three fathoms of light haze, distinctly darker on the north side of the deep water. Fred continued to snore. We returned to the pier.

Another hour passed and we prepared to make our move. I roused Fred and told him we were about to start work. Brother Norman was already on deck and ready to get underway. We would soon know if our calculations had been correct or not.

As we came alongside the Will-Glyn and breasted up (roped together) there was still an hour to go before the sky would lighten up for the break of day. The marks on the echo sounder had now increased to four fathoms of dark haze. I began to feel that familiar stir of excitement. I was now one hundred percent certain that we had done the right thing. The wing ends of the net were passed over to Brother Norman on the Will-Glyn and we began to shoot the pelagic trawl over the stern.

The net was a six-fathom square with four towing points, one on each corner, top and bottom of each side, an eighty-pound cast-iron sinker on each bottom corner with floats around the head line. Four-inch mesh made up the top square and the towing points (the wings), gradually decreasing to one-half inch in the enter and sleeve. The net is a seventy-yard-long graduated funnel, opening up like a huge mouth when the two boats separate and begin to tow. We shall be straining the water from two down to six fathoms. Hopefully, lots of sprats will be forced into the mouth of the net, and down into the enter and sleeves. The enter and sleeves are all small mesh, If we fill these with sprats, we should have nearly enough to load both boats. With a little bit of luck!

Fred lets go the stern rope first, then the head rope from the Samson post forward. The two boats come apart and begin to tow the net through the water at about two knots. The boats are now towing approximately forty yards apart. As the two boats let go of each other, Brother Norman shouts "It looks promising!"

There is now only an hour to go for the low-water. If we are going to catch any amount of fish, it will almost certainly be in the next three hours. This will be the slack tide. Once the hard flood tide comes, it is almost certain (even if there is a large shoal) that the flood tide will scatter them once more. It's a simple matter of being at the right place at the right time. The hard part is knowing exactly where that place is…

Fred comes up out of the cabin with another cup of tea and some more toast. He takes a look at the echo sounder and gives a big grin, His tongue is hanging out. He says, "Bugger! Where did they come from?"

This is the first time Fred has seen a reading like this on the echo sounder. He wants to know how thick the fish are and how many we are likely to catch. We will only know for certain when the daylight comes. It is possible to get a greatly exaggerated reading on the echo sounder in the dark or half-light. As we tow across the face of Southend Pier and the reading gets darker by the minute, I know for sure that this is a considerable shoal of fish. Already the light is showing in the eastern sky.

Switching on our radio and watching the echo sounder at the same time, I know it is time to inform Brother Ray and Brother Peter that if they have not found any fish so far, they need to come back and keep us company. Brother Peter answers my call and gives me his position. They have sounded down the middle deeps and are just crossing over into the iron bite. No sign of any large shoals so far, Just bits and pieces. I put him in the picture by telling him that we have just shot the net away on a hazy four fathoms of spots that look as though they could improve. I also tell him that he went off with my grub bag and left me without anything to eat. Peter says "Hardluck." He obviously got the message loud and clear. He now knows that we are on a very heavy reading, and expect a good catch.

Fred grins and his tongue is once more hanging out. I tell him, "Another twenty minutes, Fred. You had better get the deck ready! When the action starts, it could get a bit hectic!"

The light has spread across the dark sky as we come together and breast-up, ready to start hauling. I look astern as the winches heave in on the towing wires. Fred lets out a loud whoop. The net is already on top of the water, full and overflowing with beautiful top-quality sprats. It's the beginning of one of the best seasons ever.

Two and a half hours later, when the John Patrick and the Paul David arrive on the scene, the Dor-Bet is loaded deck-level and the Will-Glyn will be full in another ten minutes. All pulled onboard by hand, seventeen tons of shining, silver sprats.

Once more Fred's tongue is hanging out, possibly with excitement, more than likely from exhaustion. We are all dripping with sweat and covered in sprat scales!

Fred chooses this moment to remind me that today is my birthday. Saturday, the sixteenth of November. A date that will never be forgotten in my lifetime!

There is still just over an hour of this haul remaining. Fred has done extremely well in getting the fish gutted, washed, and off the deck in the two hours that we have been towing this haul. We will have plenty of time for a sandwich and a cup of tea before the routine of hauling begins again.

The weather is fine, fishing is good. Looking all around us we see that the nearest vessel in sight is several miles away, Suddenly something my father had often said (when he was with me at sea) came back to me. He would look up in the sky, then all around, and then state, "There are thousands of people that haven't got a clue where we are at this moment in time, Loll". He was probably right but we were helpless to do much about it. I often wondered what brought this on. It might have been the sun having an adverse effect. On such a day as this, with the English Channel shimmering in the burning sunshine, placid and still, all sorts of strange images could be conjured up.

Fred just walked up along the deck and came stomping into the wheelhouse. I often wondered if he missed his cockle-raking days. He always appeared to be content and we certainly didn't have many dull moments. There was always a different kind of adventure just around the corner. One in particular was most unusual and right out of the blue. As Fred handed me a cup of tea I reminded him about Fritzy and Billy Smart's circus. Fred wondered if Fritzy was still alive. We would never know.

3

We had arrived at our yard on a bright sunny morning last summer. Our intention was to go to sea. The fishing had been just a little on the quiet side and my plans for the day were a bit obscure. I had thought about going poaching for soles in Sheerness harbour, but had not yet convinced myself that it was worth the risk.

My brother Ray (who lived close by) came out to meet us with a most unusual story. My first thought was that he was pulling my leg.

He had received a telephone call from the Ministry of Fisheries office in London. The story was that Billy Smart's circus were asking for help in catching a sea lion that had escaped in the middle of a publicity stunt. They had been filming Fritzy on the deck of a hired boat and all had been going great guns until the moment that Fritzy picked up the smell of the salt water. He took one big sniff of the water and dived overboard. He was still at large despite great efforts to catch him. He was a very valuable animal, Could we help?

All of my brothers at that time were at an age where they could still enjoy something different. We all had a life that was full of adventure, but this was a challenge way outside of our normal routines—a challenge we could not refuse.

Brother Ray went back to the telephone in order to confirm that the request for help was genuine, and that we would begin to prepare for the journey up to London immediately. We were gathering together nets and other gear that we might need for this, possibly our most serious challenge ever. Brother Ray came back with the news and instructions. We would meet a contact at the Royal Festival hall in London at around twelve o'clock midday. We were to make that contact on the Thames Embankment. We began to make plans for the day, even if we did suspect that we were being conned.

We had not long purchased a diesel lorry we had named Yock's Pride, after my father and grandfather (we are all young Yocks).

We had also acquired two new ten-foot clinker-built skiffs. Our plan was to load the two skiffs onto Yock's Pride and motor up to the big city. We would also take several varied types of nets. We had no idea just what kind of challenge we were likely to encounter. We were going fully prepared for any eventuallity we could think of.

In our combined years at sea, we boasted that we had caught everything, including the kitchen sink. This was perfectly true. In one day's trawling in the upper part of the Thames, we had caught one sink, one toilet, and also an old tin bath, which completed our bathroom. All mod. cons. We had never caught or attempted to catch a sea lion. This promised to be a totally different kettle of fish.

After robbing our net store of every piece of equipment we thought might be needed and loading the equipment on board Yock's Pride, we set sail for London (in a sense)!... After making many wrong turns and getting lost twice we finally arrived on the embankment, believe it or not, in front of the Royal Festival Hall. The place was deserted.

There was a great deal of doubt in our minds as we surveyed the dirty, dark, mucky waters of the upper reaches of the Thames. Even if the information we had been given was correct, was it possible that a sea lion would be able to survive for any length of time in these murky waters?

Brother Ray and I agreed that we might need a net with more depth than any of the nets we had brought with us possessed. We decided that if we laced two Peter-nets together, it might serve our purpose.

Neither Brother Ray or myself would be considered slow with a netting needle in any company, and as we only had to lash them together roughly, this was soon done. We had just completed the task when Fred spotted a launch heading towards our position on the riverbank. At last we began to take the matter seriously, and waited with a great deal of curiosity as to what was going to happen. As yet there was no sign of the sea lion whatsoever. It was obvious that we were about to go to sea in a strange vessel. That is to say, strange to us.

Naturally both Brother Ray and myself were bursting with questions. We still had our doubts but kept them to ourselves for the moment. We waited for the skipper of the launch to put us in the picture. Never try to take command while on board a foreign ship.

The skipper received us with a big smile on his face. This was a situation which was turning into a lucrative and exciting money-making venture for the up-river boats that carried out various operations in the area. He informed us that some twenty boats were gathered on the river (full of spectators) outside the Houses of Parliament. They had Fritzy surrounded, and were not too enthusiastic for him to be caught.

With the two small skiffs in tow we headed downstream towards Westminster Bridge. The skipper was a very friendly chap and chatted away quite contentedly. He was anxious to know how we intended catching Fritzy. He looked at the box of herrings that we had brought with us and suggested that he would enjoy a feed himself if there were any left over.

We quickly put him in the picture as to how we intended to organize the capture; also that we were quite certain that the sea lion would not survive for more than two or three days this far upriver. Lack of the correct food and the close contact with many vessels would quickly put an end to his search for freedom. The skipper listened closely and agreed to give us as much help as he possibly could. He was convinced that we would not succeed in our attempt to catch Fritzy. (His comment: "You are in charge. Just keep me informed and tell me just what you want me to do.")

We had launched the two dinghies and loaded them with as much of the gear as it was safe to take with us. We were rather concerned about the bulk of equipment that would have to be left behind on the lorry (Yock's Pride). Not having the least idea what we might need caused considerable debate. It was a journey into the unknown.

There were, as far as we could determine, three nets that we might possibly use to catch Fritzy. The two Peter nets lashed together would be our first choice. This net we had already laid on the stern of one dinghy. We also had a nylon frap net that we had been experimenting with for some time. This net would only be used if we became desperate. The nylon was very strong but also very sharp and likely to cut into anything on the soft side. We certainly could not take the risk of damaging the sea lion. This net was put into the second dinghy as a third reserve.

If the Peter nets failed, our next choice would be a drag-net that we had not used for some time. My grandfather had used this net for the purpose of catching mullet, eels, and smelt, for many years. We had used the net occasionally just for a change of fishing at certain times of the year when conditions were poor for the normal methods.

This net would come in handy if we managed to trap Fritzy in shoal water. The net would be shot away with one hand remaining behind on the mud or sand (shore), holding the end of a twenty-fathom length of rope which is attached to the end of the net. The net is then rowed in a half-circle until it forms a trap around the fish. Another twenty fathoms of rope are then paid away and the end taken back to the shore and pulled in until the catch is landed.

Both dinghies are loaded with as much gear as possible without making them unseaworthy. They were being towed astern as we headed down-river towards Westminster.

If we had had any doubts about the existence of Fritzy, they were soon dispelled as we came close to Westminster Bridge. A large circle of boats crowded with spectators dominated the centre of the river. In the middle of the circle of boats was a large, sorry-looking Fritzy. He was obviously very much the worse for wear and in need of care and attention.

Fritzy ducked and dived in amongst the boats in his efforts to get at the pieces of bread that were being thrown. As he turned over and over in the water it was possible to see that he was quite seriously scarred, from coming into contact with all sorts of sharp objects. He was bleeding from two-nasty looking wounds on the top of his back. If not captured he would more than likely be dead quite soon.

Fortunately the skipper of our launch carried a loud hailer. We explained to him that we needed the circle of boats be made larger to allow us room to get the net round Fritzy. He now realized that the situation was getting out of control, and hailed the other boats accordingly. Thankfully they all complied. We were now able to get into the middle with the ferocious-looking sea lion. We asked the skipper of our launch to stand by just in case we needed assistance.

The box of herrings that we had brought with us now played a major part in our plan. We had to get Fritzy into the middle, away from all the other boats. This turned out to be quite a simple task. The moment we threw the herrings into the correct position for our needs, Fritzy became putty in our hands, He lunged towards them and once they were in his mouth he appeared to swallow them whole. Fred kept the sea lion occupied with the herrings while Brother Ray and I shot the net round him.

As we closed in with the net, Fritzy stopped feeding and took a good look at the circle of floats which now surrounded him. This was the moment that we had expected him to dive. To our complete astonishment, he rose up out of the water and leapt over the floats and head-line, clearing them by at least three feet. He was obviously a performing sea lion and appeared to be taking the mickey out of us.

Fred got to work with the herrings again and we shot the net for the second time. Fritzy was ready! Once more he approached the floats and prepared to make his leap for freedom. At the same time as he made his leap Brother Ray and I lifted the head-line up and over his head some four feet in the air. Fritzy's leap was too late.

We pulled on both the top and bottom lines, trapping the sea lion in the slack net and wrapping him up in a parcel. It needed four of us to pull him aboard!

As we lifted him aboard the launch, Fred kept feeding him with herrings until his trainer arrived on the scene and took command. Fred breathed a sigh of relief when the trainer relieved him of a very dangerous job. The sea lion was by far the most vicious catch we had ever made, and probably the most valuable single "fish."

After landing Fritzy onto some pontoons at Westminster where he was properly fed and returned to his cage and partner, we met Billy Smart for the first time. The whole family were invited as special guests to attend a gala performance of the circus on the following Saturday, with Max Bygrave playing the ringmaster. We would also be receiving a cheque for two hundred pounds. It had turned out to be a really successful day—and a most unusual catch!

We hired a coach for the special occasion and the whole family and firm, skippers, mates, wives, girlfriends all went to the circus. We had the satisfaction of observing Fritzy being licked better by his partner, and a very good time was had by all.

We named the two dinghies Fritzy One and Fritzy Two.

4

We had now settled into a steady routine of shooting and hauling the gear. Our last haul yielded a good selection of mixed fish, most of it being good quality with very little discard. Lack of small fish and general rubbish, which we just accept as normal in the Thames, contributes a great deal to a very relaxed attitude in the way we have to work on the deck: a distinct lack of urgency in getting the discard back over the side. Almost everything is saved and goes into the boxes, ready to be gutted and washed. Trawling in the Channel is very different from trawling in the Thames.

As the day quickly passes it is my intention to gradually tow our way back towards Folkestone. I need to speak to Brother Peter (on the Paul David) to determine how long he intends to stay at sea. I am reluctant to break radio silence, just in case we are being monitored by listeners ashore. It is not difficult to listen in on the trawler band on treble 2-6 or 2-3-0-6. There are many silent listeners, as I have found to my cost in the past. Providing we continue to tow in an easterly direction we should meet up with Brother Peter in the next four hours. We will then be getting close to the time that I intend landing, if all goes well.

Almost five hours and two hauls later, we are now only about one hundred yards away from the Paul David. We are both hauling for the last time today and have determined this by sign language. We have worked together for such a long time and over so many years that it would at times appear we can read each other's minds.

Fifteen minutes later the two boats come alongside each other and breast up. There is a great deal to talk about but most of this will have to wait until later. The most important objective at the moment is to make a landing and get our combined catch on the market before it closes for the day. We will have to hop about a bit smartish, Brother Peter comments, as we jog slowly towards the harbour. It will take about forty minutes to clear the last haul off the deck, cleaned, washed, and into boxes ready for the market. By that time we should be alongside the slip-way.

As we enter the harbour our attention is focused on the area that makes up the market and quay. We are hoping that there will not be an unwanted reception committee from the military. But (thank goodness) everything appears normal. It will be some time before we venture onto the Ranges again.

Landing the fish in sheltered waters is such a simple operation. We off-loaded our catch onto the slip-way and within twenty-five minutes it was sold. Having a harbour as a safe haven to return to, especially when you have experienced a very rough fishing trip, is something I always appreciate when working away from my hometown of Southend-on-Sea. I was always a little puzzled as to why my family had settled there in the first place. There were virtually no facilities for vessels of our size and needs.

I stayed aboard the boats to wash down and tidy up. Brother Peter, Fred, and Arthur, with a little bit of assistance from some of the locals, took the catch up the slip-way and to the market. I was still a little nervous that we might get a visit from the military. The quicker the fish were landed and the boats back to the barge where where we moored, the better. Once this was accomplished we could relax.

Having arrived at the barge without any problems, we could now plan for the next two days. We were coming up to the weekend and would need to plan accordingly. It was our intention (if possible) to go home for the two days. As the next day was Friday, we decided that we would just go to sea for a top tide. This would only give us about five hours' fishing (two hauls), but it will give us time to get some much-needed sleep and a good meal. We got washed and changed, and headed for the Ark Café. We would now have time to talk and make plans. One of our main problems now was to arrange transport home. As it happened, this kind of took care of itself.

When we arrived at the Ark, Fred had his usual confrontation with Big Mabel. We were rather surprised to find Bert Read and Val Noakes still sitting in their usual corner. We joined them and left the ordering to Fred.

We chatted away the time while we enjoyed our meal. There was always so much to talk about when fishermen came together in relaxed surroundings. It was an occasion that did not occur too often. There were many stories to tell, most of them true, some a little bit exaggerated, all of them interesting. Our problem of transport was about to be resolved.

Bert Read owned a very attractive-looking vessel named the Fair-Chance. She was a nice little ship. I say little, but she was bigger than the Dor-Bet and a very efficient vessel. Bert and Val had a good relationship. Val worked the Fair-Chance most of the time, but they often worked together. Bert also had an interest in a rock-making business. He owned a little green van that was used to deliver the rock to the many sweet shops that existed around Folkestone. Bert suggested that we might borrow the van for the weekend as he would not be needing it. All that needed doing was an adjustment to the brakes, which would only take five minutes. This we could do when we were ready to go home. We most gratefully accepted. A great deal was to happen before this plan came to fruition.

We stayed in the Ark chatting for more than three hours. Eventually we made our way back to the boats. Before turning in for the night, we made our plan for the next day. It would appear that things were working out quite nicely. It was time to turn in.

When I came on deck the following morning, it was about an hour after daybreak. Much to my surprise, there was a strong southwest wind. The forecast had been fresh winds, but this was a little more than fresh and could upset all our well-made plans. Brother Peter was also awake and turning his nose up at the weather. He suggested a piece of toast and a cup of tea before we made a move to get underway, if we intended going. It had to be now, or give up our plans to go home for the weekend. We decided to make our move. We could see several of the local skippers in the harbour. We reckoned they would soon be getting under way.

We steamed out of the harbour and headed up to the west. It was our intention to shoot the gear a half an hour steam away, tow to the west for something over two hours, haul, and shoot away again, towing back towards the harbour and finish. This would make it a very short day. We had made a very good week's work and put in a lot of hours. We could afford to be a little bit generous to ourselves. The water was a little bit cloudy in colour, due to the wind. We had high hopes of a few soles. Nevertheless it was very uncomfortable motoring across the outer face of the harbour. I was very tempted to turn back, but we kept going in the hope that the wind would ease and conditions improve once we got clear of the backlash that came from the swell's hitting the face of the harbour wall. One half hour later we shot away. It was a case of do or die.

We made our first haul without any undue complications. It was very uncomfortable, but just about workable. The first haul yielded a box and a half of prime plaice and two stone of soles. Another haul back east towards Folkestone yielding a similar mixture would be just what we had hoped for. We shot away again, towing east.

With the wind behind behind her the Dor-Bet was surging ahead one minute and dropping back in a trough the next. It was a bit diabolical, to say the least. I suggested to Fred that when he had finished gutting and washing the fish, he should get shaved ready for going home as soon as we landed, I would do likewise when he had finished.

Having edged just that little bit closer to the land brought me onto ground that I have not worked before. It's only perhaps the width of the gear different, but it might just as well be a mile. I am towing in strange waters and with this amount of wind behind the Dor-Bet, it's a bit fool-hardy to say the least.

Fred finished shaving and put a bowl of hot water on the hatches for me. I was now standing behind the wheelhouse and having lathered my face, started to shave. Fred has hung the mirror on the back end of the wheel house. I was still in a position to see my visual marks east of Folkestone. We were on foreign ground but I was still towing on marks that would be used another day.

One side of my face was clean and I braced myself against the mast and prepared to shave the other. Suddenly there was an almighty bang!, followed instantly by a second. Both winch barrels had run out several inches. The Dor-Bet was free and flying before the wind. We had lost our gear and the blood was streaming down my face where I caught myself with the razor. Fred rushed up on deck and was heaving in on the winch. We both knew full well what happened. We have snapped both chain sweeps, losing everything but the otter boards, and on a day such this with the weather against us there is not much we can do about it.

I always work small shackles on the sweep chains as a safety precaution just in case we ever get pinned down in weather such as we are experiencing today. This is the first time that I have ever snapped both ends at the same time. Obviously we have wrapped the whole of the net round something quite big.

There is one other safeguard I have continued to use, which many fishermen have dis-carded. I have always worked what we call a cod-end buoy: twenty fathoms of inch-diameter rope with a white float attached. On a fine day without any tide, we might just stand a chance of retrieving the gear, but not today. We head for the harbour. Brother Peter soon follows.

This is not the first time I have lost a complete set of gear (apart from the otter boards). I will not allow the loss to spoil my weekend. It does rather lessen the success of the week, which fishing-wise had been an excellent one, and it *was* one of my favourite hand-netted efforts. All was not lost; there was still a chance that we might yet recover it.

In past years I had heard fishermen make a statement that when working on rough ground they would always use an old set of gear. My approach had always been, best net to catch the most fish, unless (of course) you just wanted to dispose of the old net.

Peter had made two reasonable hauls. This helped to soften the loss of the net somewhat. At least he had made up a fairly decent week's work in two days. Over all it had been a very successful trip down-Channel.

The Folkestone fishermen had not bothered about losing a day. They were on home ground. Val Noakes made the remark that there were plenty more days in the week, and he was dead right. They would almost certainly be at sea Saturday and Sunday, at a time when hopefully we would be at home taking it easy.

When I told Val that I had lost a net, explaining the area where it had happened and the landmarks I had been working on, he shook his head knowingly. "That's the old bomber plane that came down during the war. Many of the Folkestone people had watched it come down," he said. "I am surprised you have not come to grief on that before. You must have been close many times. Taking into consideration the amount of unknown ground you cover, we reckon you have done extremely well."

We all arrived at the Ark washed and changed and ready for dinner. Several of the local fishermen made a habit of coming out in the evening dressed in their navy blue suits and matching jumpers. Most of them wore earrings, a tradition that went back many years. My grandfather always wore one in his left ear. I never did get to know the significance of this. There were many questions that I would have liked to have asked him. These will remain un-answered. He passed away when I was only twelve years old.

Although I would not call it a thriving social life, there was a great spirit of togetherness enjoyed with the Folkestone fishermen that was quite special. I never considered myself a stranger in their company. Bert Read said the green van would be waiting for us on Saturday morning. We went back on board with the intention of trying to get a decent night's sleep. I would probably lose several more nets in my dreams.

Walking round the harbour on Saturday morning, we could see that (true to his word) Bert Reid was waiting with the green van. He always appeared to have a smile on his face. He transmitted a carefree attitude to life which I knew for certain covered a very shrewd business brain. Bert was no one's fool. The better I got to know him, the more I grew to like him. He was leaning on the little van, obviously waiting for us to arrive. "Hurry up, lads," he said. "You will miss the boat." Which might well have been true, to get home we had to cross the Graves-End ferry. It was usually crowded.

Bert was one of those people who seldom used conventional methods. Despite the fact that we were gathered in the middle of the promenade. Bert instructed us to lift the van up onto its side and he would adjust the brakes, This we proceeded to do, much to the amusement of holiday-makers that were passing. Val Noakes said, "Typical."

We piled into the van and were soon on our way, with Peter at the wheel. Possibly because he was the first of the five brothers to hold a driving licence, he had always considered himself to be the best driver. He had owned a motorbike when he was still very young. This led to many adventures, as you might imagine. The sun was warm. The van smelt of sweet sticky rock and Fred's stinking feet. Fred had a foot-rot problem. I began to dream about the past.

When I was about fifteen years of age, we were at that time shrimp-fishing with two boats. Due to the fact that there was very little demand for shrimps in the week, Father would insist that we store the shrimps in large galvanized baths, starting three days before the weekend. This usually brought about a situation where we had a considerable amount to transport up to the central railway station on a Friday evening.

On this particular Friday afternoon we had landed a good catch of shrimps, close to one hundred and fifty gallons. This plus the two hundred gallons already in store brought the total to three hundred and fifty gallons. Father had built an enormous trailer for the purpose of transporting the sacks of shrimps up to the railway station.

Father was of the opinion that it would need most of the brothers to push the trailer up the hill to the station. Brother Peter insisted that the two of us could manage. "Just leave it to us," he told Father. The other three brothers were quite happy to do so.

I had not the slightest idea what Brother Peter had in mind. As he was the senior by a little over three years, mine was not to reason why. He rolled the balls, I helped him fire them.

When all the rest of the family had disappeared off the scene, Brother Peter went to collect his motorbike (he garaged it just across in the next street), leaving instructions for me to get a piece of towing rope out of the store.

The trailer only had two wheels. If not towed behind a vehicle, it had to be balanced and this was quite difficult. I was a bit mystified as to what Brother Peter had in mind. I was not kept waiting very long. It was his intention to tow the trailer with his motorbike and to tow it backwards, with me balancing the tow-bar. I was not too keen on the idea, but we had advanced much too far into his plan to back out now. We connected the tow-rope and set off up the road. To be quite honest, it worked very well.

In order to get into the central railway station, it was necessary to cross the main high street, passing the fire station on the way. A group of firemen watched in amazement as we went charging past. I suppose it was not the most common spectacle. I was running at full speed and having serious difficulty keeping pace. They watched as we approached the high street. Here there was always a policeman on duty. Today was no exception, and he was in for a very big surprise.

Our crossing of the main street was so fast that the policeman was taken off guard. We were past and up into the railway station before he had recovered from the shock of seeing a fully loaded trailer being towed by a motorbike and a lad hanging on for dear life at the back. He might have missed us on the way in, but there was no way we were going to get past him on the way out. Peter went first, in the hope that he might slip past unnoticed without the trailer. No way. The policeman stood in the middle of the road with both hands raised in the air, a very stern look on his face, but maybe a little bit of a twinkle in his eye. He was one of the older constables who had lived in Southend-on-Sea for many years and obviously knew quite a lot of the family history.

"What the devil do you think you are doing, young Yockies!" were his first words as he glowered down at Brother Peter. "You can't tow a trailer with a motorbike."

Brother Peter's answer was quick and to the point: "We just did!"

At this the policeman burst out laughing. "I am not going to waste my time talking to you young rascals, I shall be having a word with your father!" He did, and Father was not very pleased. The motorbike was banned for two weeks.

I was brought rudely back to the present by the loud squealing of brakes. Brother Peter was attempting to slow the little green van as we came towards some traffic lights. He was not having a great deal of success and advised us to hold on tight.

The van had slowed down considerably but no way was it going to stop at the lights. We went through the crossing at about twenty miles an hour. Fortunately there was very little traffic on the road and nothing stood in our way. We continued on our journey up to Graves-End but very slowly. It turned into a most uncomfortable five-hour ride. It should have taken one and a half hours but at the speed we were travelling, a horse and cart would have been a great deal quicker. We needed fifteen yards of clear road to come to a full stop.

The atmosphere in the van was absolutely sickly. The sweet smell of the stick's of rock and the unbelievable stink of Fred's feet were getting the better of all of us. Up until this time I had been sitting in the front with Brother Peter. I changed places with Fred so that he might put his feet out of the front window (the rear of the van was totally closed in). This improved the situation considerably, but it had developed into a very warm summer's day and it was very uncomfortable to put it mildly.

After a long, arduous, and painful experience we decided that we would do best to leave the van at Graves-End, take the passenger ferry across the Thames, and catch a train to Southend. This in the long run worked out very well. There was a long line of traffic and a three-hour wait for the car ferry (which was not unusual). It is quite amazing the difficulties we are prepared to put up with in order to earn a crust. We did eventually arrive home for what was left of the weekend. We would be on our way back to Folkestone at two A.M. Monday morning. It's a hell of a life, if you enjoy that sort of thing…

We arrived back at Folkestone on the Monday morning to find everything in order. It was a beautiful daybreak with the sun coming up like a ball of fire. It was going to be a scorcher with very little wind. My mind was already on the lost set of gear. That would come up for consideration only after we had attempted to earn a day's pay.

Leaving the vessels in a strange port always carried a certain amount of risk. The responsibility of taking care of your own ship was very demanding, even more so if the ship belonged to another person, even if that person was your father.

All these thoughts ran through my mind as we steamed out of the harbour. Once again I had a plan to put into operation. It's time for that plan to begin. This is another week.

We had worked through the whole twenty four-hours since leaving the harbour yesterday morning. The fishing had been steady. Forty stone of plaice and twelve stone of soles are now gutted, washed, and boxed, ready to go on the market. It has been a successful night without any problems (thank goodness). The tide will soon be flowing into the harbour. This will be slack water and the right time to look for our lost net. Conditions are just about as good as they get. If the cod-end marker buoy is going to show, it will most certainly do so in the next hour.

I have taken care to be on the visual towing marks in plenty of time. We are now motoring very slowly, backwards and forwards, just to the seaward side of the line where we lost the net.

The last thing I want to do is pick up the marker with the Dor-Bet's propellor. Fred is sitting for'ard on the Samson, keeping a sharp lookout. We must be patient. The loss of a couple of hours is nothing compared with the value of a complete set of gear.

Because of the care I have taken in pinpointing the exact spot where we first came fast on what we now know to be a bomber plane, we only have to search an area of one hundred yards by fifty yards. The chances of success in finding the marker buoy should be more than fifty-fifty. Getting the net back aboard could be a much more difficult problem.

All these thoughts are passing through my mind as the Dor-Bet jogs slowly up and down. We are now on the third leg of our search. Fred is getting restless.

Suddenly Fred is up on his feet, pointing. He can see the white float, no more than thirty yards inside of our line and directly abreast of our position. At least we have found the cod-end marker.

As we approach the marker buoy, Fred lets go another anchor and a larger buoy, just in case we have to drag for the net. The cod-end buoy line will stand only a limited amount of strain. If we break it, we will still have another chance of recovery. Very gently we approach and pick up the cod-end buoy.

Fred keeps me informed as he takes in the slack rope. We are lying head into the last of the flood tide. It is my intention to try to drag the net away from the bomber stern-first, in the opposite direction to which we lost it in the first place.

Slowly the strain comes onto the rope and I quickly take the power off until the Dor-Bet has the full weight of the net and gear. Soon we shall know the worst.

We now have the rope extended to its maximum and tight. Fred has two turns round the Samson post and signals all is well.

It's time to use a little bit of power. I put the engine slow astern and the Dor-Bet begins to move away from the wreck of the bomber. Much to our surprise she keeps moving and the whole of the gear comes clear. Fred's thumb is in the air, his tongue is hanging out, and he has a broad grin on his face. The net has come clear of the bomber. We still have to bring it back on board and repair the damage, but not to worry. At least the operation has been a complete success. I quietly say a word of thanks. The damage turns out to be minimal.

After recovering the trawl we motored slowly towards Folkestone Harbour. Our catch is prepared and ready to go on the market. Fred is at the wheel of the Dor-Bet and for the moment, in charge. I set about unfrapping the net and the attached gear—it has all come aboard in one big heap. Nothing is missing and an hour's concentrated effort should see it back together and ready for use. There are black mud and brown rust marks on both the head rope and foot-rope. It is fairly certain that we had been very fortunate in wrapping the whole gear round the bomber plane rather than just snagging it. The way it had come clear was somewhat close to a miracle.

I had now got the gear pulled out along the whole length of the deck and could see the extent of the damage. The head-line rope is badly chafed, but not broken. Several meshes behind the head-rope will also need to be cut out and repaired. I settle down on the hatches and attack the necessary repairs. As always, my mind begins to wander.

In the spring of this same year, we had worked for long periods of time on the Kent side of the Thames. This is not unusual. I have always considered this to be my stamping ground. Possibly the greater part of my fishing life has been spent more in the middle and on the south side of the river than on the north side. Purely a figment of my imagination, but the south side always appeared to be warmer and certainly more fertile. Much of our family's fishing experiences in and after the war were carried out over a very large area stretching from the isle of Grain (going east) to the north foreland. The thought brings to mind many incidents and adventures. One was almost fatal for Fred.

5

We had been working along the Red Sand, much of the time close to the Red Sand Towers. These were constructed as part of the defences during the war. There were a considerable number of ships sunk in the area, many of them standing out above the water like tombstones as a reminder of the dark days that had gone before. But there were far more wrecks on the seabed that could not be seen. Some of these were marked on the chart, many more were not. But we had come fast or lost nets on most of these at some time or another. We had visual marks and depth soundings plus compass bearings that enabled us to keep clear most of the time. But not all of the time! This particular day was one when we did not keep clear.

There is an old saying that all the bad eggs come in one basket. This spring morning turned into a bad-egg day not to be forgotten.

We put to sea, leaving Southend at two A.M. (high-water), with a reasonably hard running tide. This should keep the water nice and thick and good for catching mixed fish even when the daylight came. We began trawling at the very top end of the Spile sand, towing towards the Red Sand Towers some six miles to the east. We had completed two hauls of an hour each and the fishing had been quite good, a mixture of plaice, soles, and skate. Prospects for the low-water haul inside the Towers (this was usually the best) were most promising. We were approaching the Towers now.

Inside the Towers there is a hole of deeper water. It's only about two fathoms more but this is where most of the fish are to be found on the low water, the crucial time being just either side of the low-water, which we call the slack tide.

On the south side of the hole is a wreck that is clearly visible for most of the tide. On the north side, three wrecks on the seabed, not visible and to be avoided at all costs.

It was my intention to tow eastwards on the north side of the hole close to one of these wrecks and turn to the south into the hole at dead low-water. This would bring us onto the best ground at the best possible time. This was my plan, and not a time to push my luck!

In simple language, I misjudged the amount of wind and tide. The fresh southwest breeze pushed us just a few yards further over to the north than I had anticipated. We came fast on one of the wrecks. This messed up the whole day.

We had winched in the net and managed to reach the wing-ends but there was too much tide to work on the gear amid-ships. We were forced to take the wing-ends for'ard. We already had a good thick strop made fast (tied) round both wing-ends. Everything was under control. Fred had the strop made fast—two turns round the Samson post. I was ready to use some engine power in an effort to break clear. Suddenly Fred signalled me to wait. He had managed to pull in some more slack net, He took the turns off the Samson post and attempted to pull. This left him badly exposed without any ropes made fast.

He had only managed to pull in a small amount of slack net when the tide took complete control of the Dor-Bet, pulling the net back overboard, and Fred went with it, his legs caught up in the wing-ends.

I am quite certain that if the net had not come clear of the wreck at that precise moment, Fred would have gone down tangled up in the wing-ends. As it was, one of the end chains gave him a nasty clout on the head. Fortunately he remained conscious and we still had the sweeps made fast amid-ships. With my heart in my mouth and a great deal of strain on my arms I managed to pull him back on board. This was as close to a disaster as I ever wanted to get!

"What madcap scheme are you dreaming up now, Skipper?" Fred's grinning face poked out of the back of the wheelhouse.

"I was just mopping your bleeding brow, inside the Red-Sand Towers!" I replied.

"Never mind mopping my bleeding brow inside the Towers; stay away from those bloody tracer shells on the Ranges. If you go in there again, I shall be taking sick leave." We both laughed and I suggested that the military had probably run out of shells anyway. Fred said that the Montgomery was full of them, they would never run out. I carried on with my repairs.

Fred's reference to the ammunition ship that sank just outside Sheerness Harbour set my mind off on another tack. She had become something of a legend. Hardly a week would go by in Southend-on-Sea without the question of the Montgomery being discussed by somebody. Was she dangerous or not?

The Montgomery is an American Liberty ship that moored in the wrong position just about a mile northeast of Sheerness Harbour. When the tide ebbed she sat on a sandbank (known as the the Sheerness middle ground). She broke her back and sank. The ship was reputed to be full of explosives capable of blowing both Southend and Sheerness into Kingdom Come if she went up.

The ship had sunk only about three hundred yards to the north of the main channel into Sheerness. At this point in time her masts, spars, and bridge were visible at high water even on the biggest tides. There was no doubt whatsoever that she was a danger to shipping, with or without the threat of explosives. One way or another she would always remain a problem for discussion.

In the latter part of the war and for some time afterwards, we trawled for shrimps on both the south side and the north side of the ship, passing so close to her that at times I wondered if we would ever catch her anchor and cable, but it had never happened. The chances are that they were buried in the sand. The whole ship would almost certainly disappear in time, perhaps a long time, but it would happen. It was decided that the ship was too dangerous to move.

Over the years (as the ship gradually broke into several pieces), our family had trawled up many shell-heads from close around the ship. We assumed that these came out of the ship. I had caught many dud heads, but nothing alive and dangerous from that area. But plenty from elsewhere!

6

The two eldest brothers (Raymond and Bramwell) had returned from the navy and joined the firm, as we called the family business. The war had just ended and I was in the first year of what was to be my apprenticeship. Most of this would be spent in the eighteen-foot open-boat Peter-net skiff in the company of brother Ray, eleven years my senior and already an experienced fisherman. It was to prove a very good partnership, but the first winter was extremely hard in an open boat. It was a crash course of endurance for both of us.

We were trawling with a small-mesh beam trawl designed specifically for catching shrimps. It would catch other fish, but the water had to be thick (stirred up, dirty, sandy). The beam was the same length as the boat we were working. It was a bit crowded, to say the least.

One of our relations in Leigh-on-Sea had borrowed our largest vessel during the war. At this time we had to make the best of a bad job with two small boats, The largest of these had been named after my eldest sister (The Lady Doreen). She carried the boiling copper and was responsible for the cooking of all the shrimps caught by both boats. She was crewed most of the time by Brother Bram and Brother Norman. If Father came to sea, I would make third hand on either vessel if they had more work than they could cope with. It worked reasonably well most of the time. It was no problem for me as I had a very good working relationship with all of my brothers. I was that much younger and didn't get involved in any decision-making at that time.

One very fine early spring morning we had put to sea one and a half hours after high-water (one and a half-hour's ebb). We had successfully dodged the shipping while crossing the main channel (called sea reach), it being our intention to work on an area of ground called the West Shore. It was actually the east end of the Isle of Grain. We would go right into the mouth of Sheerness Harbour (on the west side) and trawl out towards the Montgomery. We were trawling for brown shrimps. It was one of our best yielding grounds and we would most likely make two turns on the west shore (waiting for the tide to ease) and then tow east towards the sunken ship Montgomery, keeping her on our port side.

As so often happens at sea, the weather changed our plans. We had completed one turn towing out and then towing back (in slightly deeper water) so that we did not tow over the same ground twice. As we turned to tow back out for the second time, daybreak came and dense fog closed in. This was not unexpected. It was a flat calm without a breath of wind. We had now to decide if it was worth the risk of towing east towards the sunken ship or staying safely on the west shore. We knew full well that staying on the west shore for the whole tide would decrease our over-all catch. Brother Ray decided we would make one more turn and then tow east. Perhaps by that time the fog would clear.

Far from clearing, if anything the fog became even thicker. Visibility was down to just a few yards and with nothing to look at it was impossible to tell just how far you could see. We decided to take the risk and head east towards the sunken ship.

Our situation at this particular time in the history of our family is almost impossible to describe in ordinary terms to the satisfaction of landlubbers.

The Peter-net skiff's engine is a Kelvin sleeve, petrol-paraffin four-cylinder, and very old. With a little bit of luck! We start the engine each morning with petrol and change over to paraffin when the engine is heated enough to take it, then switch back to petrol again before stopping the engine. If this procedure is not followed religiously, the spark plugs will oil up and the engine cease to function.

We are towing towards the Montgomery and we will soon be hauling. The net has now been in the water three hours. Brother Ray says it is time we had a look. He switches the engine over to petrol in preparation for reducing power because it is not reliable on paraffin. We stand in the stern cockpit of the skiff (in line, one behind the other) and begin to pull. The whole process is hand-operated; we have not advanced enough to install a winch. If we lack the necessary strength to manhandle the eighteen-foot wooden beam and net, then it stays on the sea-bed until we can get assistance, a most unsatisfactory situation. We begin to pull.

It is always a physical challenge to haul and get the net aboard but we manage this without too much difficulty. When we eventually reach the cod-end, it is to find that there are more shrimps than we can pull on board in one go. They have to be halved and although this is not a problem, it will take time. Brother Ray decides to switch the engine off.

With the engine running, we are deaf. The fog being dense, we are more or less blind. Unless one has experienced these conditions and how they affect the mind, one would not understand the unbelievable silence once the engine is switched off.

It is taking us some time to sort the twenty-three gallons of shrimps. There are several bits and pieces of rubbish and small fish to pick out before we can put them into boxes, mainly polly-wigs or white-throats, as we call them. We can faintly hear the engine of one other vessel some distance away, thankfully not close enough to cause us any concern. It would appear that we have the immediate surrounding area to ourselves. But not quite.

We have had our head's down working on the shrimps for close on forty minutes. What is left of the ebb tide is very slowly taking us further eastward. We are not concerned. If another vessel should come our way we are bound to hear it. We work away at the shrimps contentedly.

A sudden bump shatters our contentment. Absorbed as we are in our work, we have completely forgotten the Montgomery. We have run into one of her masts, bits and pieces of the wreck are showing above the water within a few feet. Hitting the mast has not caused any damage, but a jagged piece of wreckage just under the surface of the water could quite easily tear out the boat's bottom. We hold our breath and for some reason begin to whisper to each other. I can't believe that any of the crew are still aboard, but we are taking no chances.

It strikes me as rather ironic that my two elder brothers have been away from home serving in the Navy for six years, the war is finished, and here we are back in a war situation, a sunken ship surrounding us like a graveyard.

Fortunately, there is not a ripple on the surface of the sea so the danger is not as great as it might be. The moment we had come into contact with the ship's mast, Brother Ray had hopped over the thwart (seat) and grabbed it. He was now laid over the side of the skiff and hanging on for dear life. But there was no sign of any panic. He knew exactly what he was doing. We had come into the danger area one way, we needed to go out that same way. He was holding the boat in the same position. We had to avoid coming into contact with anything else, especially if that contact was under the water.

I had reached under the stern thwart and grabbed the rowlocks. Taking them right for'ard I shipped the ten-foot-long oars (which we always carried) and waited for instructions. I knew for certain there was no way we would attempt to start the engine. If only half the rumours we had heard were true we were sitting on a virtual time bomb.

The tide had more or less stopped. It was dead low-water. That much was definitely in our favour. Without dipping the oars any deeper than I was forced, in order to get the weigh on the skiff, I brought her head round until she was heading west, back the way we had come from. Brother Ray let go of the mast and motioned me to keep going. I needed no second bidding. The further we were away from the Montgomery the better. But the day was still young yet. We needed to catch more shrimps.

Once we were completely clear of the sunken ship, Brother Ray started the engine. Heading north and working the lead-line we deepened the water into the lower end of the swatch-way. We shot the net away once more and headed east. We would tow in this direction for fifty minutes. Sometime during the day we had to find The Lady Doreen in order to get the shrimps cooked. There was never a dull moment.

At last the sun broke through the fog and it began to lift. A couple of miles to the east we could see The Lady Doreen. She was towing in our direction and belching black smoke from her copper funnel. It appeared that Brother Bram had just stoked up the boiler fire in preparation for cooking our catch. He was going to be quite busy for several hours. We had already been at sea for more than six hours but there was a long time to go yet.

When we eventually arrived back at Southend later that day, Father was waiting for the shrimps. It was Friday and the most important day of the week where Father was concerned. It was weekend customer day and he was waiting to transport the catch to all points of the compass. But first he would satisfy his local customers, waiting in a an orderly queue on the seawall. I always believed this was one of Father's greatest pleasures in life. He was a master salesman. He also informed us that we would be going Peter-net fishing on Monday. The London market for shrimps had taken a tumble, which was no surprise, seeing that there were more than thirty boats fishing for shrimps in the River Thames at that time. Tomorrow we would be getting the Peter-nets and anchors out of the store. This was great news.

Monday morning I was up and ready an hour before high-water. First time for the spring Peter-net season had always been exciting when I was at school. This was my first trip as a professional. It was now April and I had left school last Chistmas. I am now fourteen and a half years of age and raring to go. Father will be coming to sea with us. We shall be three-handed in the Peter-boat skiff. I have the boat in alongside the jetty, waiting for Father and Brother Ray to arrive. It is two A.M. and a beautiful morning. We shall soon be off.

We manage to cross the shipping channel safely, despite the number of ships underway. Only making five knots maximum, we sometimes have to wait a considerable time before we can dodge between them. With a three-knot tide behind them, they can be making as much as sixteen knots. They do not give way to anyone.

Father is in charge of the boat while we lay the nets on the stem ready to shoot. Ray looks after the foot line, which is weighted. I take care of the head-line and the floats. Father has a long tiller to steer with and that keeps him out of our way. Everything is going nicely. We are just passing Warden Point on our starboard side, bound for Ham-Gat and the Columbine spit. The sun is just breaking over the horizon and everything looks perfect. With a little bit of luck we should arrive in position to shoot the nets in plenty of time.

Father turns round to survey the heap of nets on the stern. He comments that they would go overboard more easily if they were further out over the stern. We stay silent. It is much too early in the morning for an argument and the job is nearly finished. We are just on the last of the twelve nets when the engine makes a strange sound. It does not sound happy! Suddenly it screams then grinds to a stop. Ceased solid! It would appear that our little bit of luck just ran out!

True to form, Father took out his handkerchief and gave a hard blow. He looked at Brother Ray, either for guidance or hoping for some sort of miracle. The fact that he did not come to sea that often made the engine Brother Ray's responsibility, I was shipping the oars. Brother Ray's only comment: "Dad, I think you just got your answer." I had shipped the oars and was pulling hard towards the ground where we intended shooting the nets. The thought of rowing all the way home without even attempting to fish was totally unacceptable.

It would take us perhaps thirty or forty minutes to reach Ham-Gat. I was sitting in the usual position (on the for'ard thwart) for rowing. Brother Ray was quick to join me, putting his considerable weight behind the oars. All of my brothers are very strong, The heavy skiff began to move through the water much faster.

Father blows his nose once again as he takes a good look round at the sky. He is assessing the weather and what might happen later in the day. He can find very little to complain about. It looks like being a beautiful day. He states that as soon as we start to deepen the water, he will take over the oars and we will shoot the nets; otherwise we are going to be late. Father always rows the nets out. He is a very accomplished oarsman.

We have almost reached our destination. Father has been sounding the depth of water with the sounding pole for the last five minutes. He signals that he is ready to take over the oars. We all change places and the nets begin to run out over the stern. Brother Ray keeps his eye on the nets. I throw the anchors overboard each time we come to the end of a net. Twelve nets, fifteen anchors, and six marker floats in seven minutes. At last we are fishing, even if it is a long row home.

The moment the last anchor and marker float have gone overboard, Father turns the skiff into the tide and I let go the skiff's anchor. It is now time for a sandwich and a cup of tea. Father looks at the line of floats and nods his satisfaction. When the tide comes round and through the nets (on the last of the tide) they will be as near perfect as can be. We now have almost two hours to wait. The nets are shot and straining the water in a depth of seven feet. If all goes well, we shall be hauling in a depth of about three feet. We cross our fingers and everything else and hope for the best. It is all in the lap of the gods. I say a quiet word.

Although it will be more than an hour before we begin to haul the nets, this is no time to idle. The skiff has to be completely clear of water (in the bilges). There will be lots of water coming aboard with the nets, even if they are clear of dirt and weed.

Fishing from a small boat such as the skiff, everything has to be routine and well prepared. There is no margin for error or mistakes. The whole operation has to be carried out at the right time and in the correct way. Every fifteen minutes, Father picks up the sounding pole and checks on how fast the tide is dropping (ebbing) and also how fast the tide is running. If the tide slows or stops suddenly, it is possible that any fish that are in the nets can swim along to the ends (pockets) and if the water clears, may swim out.

Today the conditions appear to be perfect. There is a good, hard running tide and the water is a nice sandy brown colour. Each time Father sounds with the pole, the depth has decreased by approximately ten inches. Brother Ray is working on the engine. He is not very hopeful.

I have been standing up on the thwart for some time looking along the line of nets. It is often possible to see the fish waking.

Quite often the skate will hit the net and come to the surface for a few seconds, or even stay on the top of the water if there is a great deal of tide running. We have to be ready at a moment's notice. When Father says "Haul!" we haul.

We are a little disappointed that there does not appear to be much sign of life along the nets. Although I did think that I had seen a couple of wakes further along towards the centre. Twelve fifteen-fathom nets is a long stretch of gear. Father tells me there is still a four-foot depth of water and that there is plenty of time. He says I am too impatient. Brother Ray closes the engine case and shaking his head, says there is not much he can do to the engine until he has more time. We relax for a further twenty minutes. The depth of water has decreased to three feet and we prepare to haul. Father ships the oars while I attend to the anchor. Brother Ray stands ready to pick up the first marker buoy (Dan-buoy).

As brother Ray pulls and seesaws up and down in his efforts to pull the first anchor out of the seabed, Father suggests that we are likely to have a good pull recovering the nets today. The tide is not going to ease. It is now coming from the southeast, as opposed to the southwest when we first shot the nets. It is still running quite strong.

At last the first anchor comes away from the seabed and aboard. Brother Ray is now pulling on the lines. I will take in the slack net and pull the fish aboard. If any.

The pocket of the net is pulling straight down, something I have not experienced before. Father says, "Pull, Loll: There is a fish sanded up in the pocket." I put all my weight on the slack net (lint). With a loud sucking noise the first enormous skate comes over the side. It must weigh well over twenty pounds and there are another fourteen in the first net. They are all female fish and the largest I have ever seen. If we continue along all the nets with the same average, Father expresses the doubt that the skiff will not be big enough to carry them all. We haul the first set, four nets.

Father tells me to pick up the marker buoy for the next set of gear and we hang on the rope. It is our intention to clear a couple of the nets that have come aboard so far, in order to get some of the fish into the little boat's bows. We have to spread the weight evenly, to give us any hope of getting the remaining eight nets on board. We have to hurry.

After a long, hard struggle, we have recovered all twelve nets and the little skiff is deep-loaded. That has been the hardest pull of my working life so far. We have cleared four nets of the skate and the fish have been stowed in the bows. The skiff is still dangerously low at the stern. Father takes out his handkerchief and gives one almighty blow. Somehow I cannot see that this is going to help, but it appears to give him time to think; possibly it is a substitute for pulling his hair out.

I am already clearing the anchors from the net-ends and stowing them on either side of the engine case. Father stops me in full flow. He has other plans for me.

"Make yourself as comfortable as possible on the for'ard thwart, Loll. You fancy yourself as an oarsman, now is the time to convince us. Ship the oars and start rowing. The tide is behind you all the way and is coming from the southeast. You need to be off into the four-fathom channel in time to carry the full flood tide (from the east) all the way home to Southend. Keep your eyes open for any steamboat's swell or any other movement more than a ripple. At the moment it is a flat calm and we have to pray that it stays that way. Any movement whatsoever, bring her bows into it and hold her steady." I begin to row. And row. And row! Six hours later I am still rowing…

It has taken us six and a half hours and we are just inside the west Shoebury buoy. We have just been taken in tow by *The Lady Doreen*. My backside is numb and my shoulders ache. I am fortunate that my hands are now hard as leather from constant pulling on the shrimp trawl ropes. I will survive.

We had one or two very anxious moments crossing the shipping lanes. Father instructed me to try to cross the two Channels just west of the Nore Towers, which I had managed to do. Each time a ship passed, I brought the skiff round, head to the wash that followed. One ship much larger than the others caused such a swell, the skiff almost dipped her stern under. She shipped so much water that Father and Brother Ray stopped what they were doing and grabbed buckets! They bailed furiously for five minutes. It was a very close shave with disaster. We carried no life jackets of any description.

Father and Brother Ray had been working at clearing the nets and cleaning the fish. The skiff was now fairly stable and seaworthy but very low in the water; Her bilges were running red with blood and skate livers. Our catch amounted to one hundred and fifty of the largest fish Father had ever seen landed. Every skate was a female in prime condition. It was not possible to pick up any one of the fish without using two hands.

We had just managed to carry the last of the tide all the way home, but there was still another two hours' work getting the catch ashore and into boxes. It had been a long, hard day, but a very exciting day, to say the least.

In the time that Father had been washing the fish, Brother Ray had managed to free the engine. He had come to the conclusion that the sea-cock on the bottom of the boat had become blocked with weed. This had caused the engine to overheat and cease. We would be ready and fit for sea the next day.

It was the normal procedure to hang the Peter-nets out to dry on the jetty just east of the pier. Father said not to bother, by the time we arrived at our home in Myrtle Road and had a bite to eat and a few hours' sleep it would be time to set out once more. Life was hard but never dull.

As we had been coming up past the Mulberry harbour on the way home, we had received a cheer from the cockle fleet as they motored past us on their way into Leigh-on-Sea. The Osbournes, Meddles, Denches, all stopped and asked if we wanted a tow. We were more worried about the wash they created than anything else. We thanked them and said we would wait for The Lady Doreen to take us in tow. She would be less likely to sink our poor little skiff.

When my head hit the pillow that night I was tired, to say the least. Not too tired to wonder when we were going to get the Reindeer back from our relations in Leigh-on-Sea. Today was a clear indication of how much we needed her. It was not possible to keep running the risks and getting away with them as we had been. I would ask Father in the morning. I closed my eyes and dreamed of much bigger fishing ships…

"Shall I take her in or have you finished planning tomorrow's adventures?" Fred is an excellent mate but shows very little interest in skippering a vessel of any kind. We are just passing the harbour wall and the net is repaired ready for use once more. The Paul David is coming along-side with the intention of breasting up. We shall land together.

I am quite happy to work alone at Folkestone or anywhere else, for that matter, but it is nice to have some support if anything should go wrong. We quickly land our catch and make for the Ark Café. We are now a permanent part of the scene and are soon wading through a huge plate full of seven different varieties of food. Val Noakes suggests that I would do better if I had several plates. He has never seen one person eat so much food. Soon the stories begin to flow.

Val had landed early. He had steamed very slowly into the harbour with his net still hanging overboard. The Fair-Chance had come fast on an object that was so big and heavy, they were unable to bring it to the surface. Val had a very strong suspicion that it could be a contact mine or a torpedo. But they would have to wait for the tide to ebb out of the harbour to find out. This would take at least another four hours.

Val asked if we had heard any news of Candy or Lord Edward. Brother Peter pricked his ears up. He had not been told about the Neptune. Val said we should have claimed salvage.

The mention of salvage stirred up all sorts of memories. Brother Peter reminded me of one occasion before Fred had joined the Dor-Bet. In fact it was in the days of the old Reindeer, when Belgie Joe and Brother Norman were with us.

We had put to sea in the Reindeer, leaving Southend-on-Sea at one A.M. and punching quite a stiff easterly breeze. We were bound for the Maplin Sands, Peter-net fishing and towing two skiffs. We were four-handed (four in the crew).

There had been a certain amount of reluctance when we had first turned out. We expected the easterly wind to drop with the tide but there were no guarantees. Whatever, it was going to be a very uncomfortable two-hour steam to reach the Maplin Buoy.

We decided that we would not attempt to get the nets ready until we reached our destination, which was just as well. On this particular day we never put a net in the water.

Brother Peter and Brother Norman had never been too happy at punching into an easterly wind so early in the morning. They were sitting behind the wheelhouse drinking their tea. They were of the opinion that we would have been better off to stay at home. At the moment I was inclined to agree with them.

It would be another ten minutes before we would arrive on the grounds we intended to work. At regular intervals the swell came crashing over the top of the wheelhouse. It was not very pleasant, to say the least.

Belgie Joe was keeping a sharp lookout through the front window. There should not be anything in our path but it was always wise to expect the unexpected. Joe could see a light where to all intents and purposes there should not be one. And it was even more curious that the light was not steady, it was inconsistent, one moment bright, the next fading. We would have to investigate even if it did mean steaming past the Maplin buoy. The light, which turned out to be a distress flare, was two miles to the east of our position and appeared to be on the east end of the Maplin spit, which ebbs a-dry. With a strong easterly wind over an ebb tide, this was not a very good position to be in, as we were soon to find out.

There was one thing in our favour, There was the first hint of daybreak in the eastern sky. It was now possible to see the white-topped waves as they rolled up the Swin towards us. We slowly approached the vessel that was in distress.

It was now possible to see two crewmen standing in the cockpit of a fifty-foot-long motor cruiser. They were feeding a fire on top of the large cabin hatch and using oily rags for fuel. The yacht towered above the Reindeer as we came within haling distance. I would not risk going alongside until we found out what the situation was, I would leave that to Brother Peter and Brother Norman. The yacht was anchored in three fathoms of water and safe for the moment, so far as we could tell. Brother Peter was speaking to them. We would soon find out.

I had that strange feeling that life was going to get complicated. If the yacht was in serious trouble, we would be forced to find some sheltered water for the two skiffs. We could offer very little assistance with the two skiffs towing astern. Brother Peter came into the wheelhouse for a conference. Brother Norman could be heard still shouting above the noise of the wind. The weather was not improving.

The fifty-foot-long yacht was new and only just off the slipway, out of Burnham and bound for the Medway. The skipper had tried to cut the corner across the top of the Maplin spit and had run the yacht aground. She was making water (leaking). They could not tell how bad the leak was but the last time they had checked in the engine room there had been almost three feet of water in the well. The two brand-new Kelvin diesels were half under water. The skipper and his mate had endured a very uncomfortable night and wanted to be taken off. We had to make a quick decision. Any delay could only increase the problems that faced us. Fishing was now out of the question. We decided to take them off.

Brother Norman came up with the suggestion that he take the two skiffs into the shallow water and jog slowly towards home. Now that it was coming lighter all the time, we would be able to keep an eye on him. This we agreed.

After he had departed, we put every fender we possessed on the Reindeer's port side and prepared to take the yacht's crew off. This was achieved with less difficulty than we had expected. It appeared that at last the wind and the swell had begun to ease a little. Joe gave the two men a cup of tea. Brother Peter asked them what action they wanted us to take. Their answer was that they could not care less, we could do as we pleased. It had been a very bad night. We decided to wait an hour and then survey the situation afresh.

The wind continued to drop away. It was far from a calm but it was improving all the time. As the tide began to ease so the swell eased with it. We decided to attempt to salvage the vessel.

We had been observing the yacht from a distance of some fifteen yards. She did not appear to be making any amount of water. I put the Reindeer on her starboard side. Brother Peter jumped aboard, and Joe soon followed. I stood off while they took stock of the problems that we were about to face. Brother Peter went into the wheelhouse and disappeared down below. I kept the Reindeer close handy just in case. After twenty minutes Joe put up his thumb. I could go alongside.

It was obvious that the Reindeer would not be able to tow the yacht abreast with the quite heavy swell that continued to roll up the Swin. I put the Reindeer alongside and Joe jumped aboard with ropes ready to make fast but I knew it was not possible for me to remain there in that position. Brother Peter came on deck. We had a quick discussion.

It appeared that the yacht was still making water (leaking) but not impossible to deal with. He needed tools for a number of reasons which he did not go into. I handed over my fish box full of well-oiled tools. I had purchased these when I had become skipper of the Reindeer the previous year, when I was just eighteen years old. I guarded them jealously. My brothers were notorious for losing or breaking tools.

Brother Peter had some serious problems to deal with. The engine pumps were all under water. Whoever had had the boat built had not bothered to install hand-operated bilge pumps. A bucket was useless, he needed a bigger container and was going to cut part of the top off of a five-gallon drum. He would fill the drum from the engine room. Then Joe would pull it up on a rope and tip it on the deck. The water could then run overboard.

There was a serious mechanical problem. For some reason the rudder was locked in a hard-over-to-starboard position. He had tried but could not move it.

As he was speaking to me, the yacht rolled onto the Reindeer's top gunwale, breaking three timberheads. I had to keep clear and attempt to tow her astern, however difficult! We were in danger of doing some serious damage. I let go and moved ahead, taking the tow rope with me.

Joe had made the tow rope fast on a bollard on the yacht's starboard bow. This would go some way to overcome the rudder problem, I was towing from the bottom of the Reindeer's mast. The mast was situated well forward of mid-ships, just behind the wheelhouse. This gave me more control. It was far from perfect, but for the moment it would serve our purpose. I headed for the shallows inside and west of the Maplin buoy. I also kept a sharp eye out for any signals from Joe. It was going to be a long, demanding day!

The yacht had a draft of well over six feet. This prevented me from going in too close to the sand, which was now well dried out. Progress was slow but ongoing. We were making about three knots. I had the satisfaction of seeing Brother Norman way up to the west with the two skiffs. He was almost up to the Blacktale spit and by this time in calm waters.

I could see the figure of Belgie Joe bobbing up and down at regular intervals. The water must be coming out of the bilge at a fair lick. Only an hour had passed but I could already see that the yacht was no longer wallowing. She must have lifted almost twelve inches. We were just about to enter the smooth water and comparative safety. Everything was gradually coming under control.

Brother Peter had just come up on deck and signalled for us to breast up. We were now making far better headway and carrying the first of the flood tide. The Blacktale spit buoy was just outside of our present position as the two boats came together. I could see that Brother Peter had a bloody rag wrapped around his thumb. He had snagged his thumb on the rough sharp edge of the five-gallon bailing drum. He waved away my concern. The wound was not serious and everything was ship-shape and under control.

We breasted up the two boats alongside each other and settled down for a break and a cup of tea. Joe made some bacon sandwiches.

Brother Peter was content that the yacht was safe until we reached Southend Pier. This was some two hours' away at our present speed. It was his intention to borrow a motor pump from the lifeboat house. At this point in time he was second coxswain of the lifeboat. The whole situation was looking a little brighter.

The yacht's crew came on deck. They had been asleep in the Reindeer's cabin throughout the whole drama. They were now fully recovered and tucked into the tea and sandwiches offered by Joe.

From that moment on everything went very smoothly. We arrived at the pier two hours later and laid in alongside the lifeboat slip-way. The pump was quickly hoisted onto the yacht's deck and went straight into action. In twenty minutes the vessel was clear of water. We had also managed to free the rudder on our way up to the pier.

Peter agreed to make out a report for the piermaster and take care of the formalities. He had a signed statement from the yacht skipper. His thumb also needed medical attention.

Once more the Reindeer took the yacht in tow bound for Rochester. I settled down, content that the worst was over and that Joe was there to back me up if we encountered any problems.

We reached Rochester just in time to hand over the yacht and catch the ebb tide back out of Sheerness harbour on the return passage. I wondered what Father would say about the three broken timberheads. The damage could have been much greater!

The Ark was crowded with a mixture of fishermen and holiday makers. It was a meeting place where one could always hear a good story. They flowed thick and fast.

Val Noakes had everybody sitting on the edge of their seats. He was telling about the time when he came into the harbour with an enormous contact mine standing on the deck. It had taken about four hours to get the mine aboard, and another hour to get it clear of the net.

The harbour master had gone completely up the wall when he saw the mine sitting on the deck of the Fair-Chance in the middle of the harbour. A bomb disposal squad was hurried aboard and they motored off into the middle of the English Channel, where it was detonated.

Val was quite certain that the obstacle that they were waiting to inspect, once the tide had left the harbour, was a large rock. The ground where they had been trawling was close in under the cliffs off Dover and notorious for the number of rocks that had been landed by many fishing vessels over the years. He complained that mine crates were one of the most damaging relics left over from the war. These were metal frames that were made to protect the mines when dropped from aircraft. I could sympathise with him, I had caught two myself and they caused a considerable amount of damage to the net.

As we sat in the comfort of the Ark talking about the amount of debris that came up in the nets, I wondered if the general public had any idea just how much very expensive rubbish was lost and abandoned during the course of a six-year war. Looking round at the number of fishermen gathered in the Ark at this moment, I could not even imagine the value of weapons and materials that they would have recovered in the past twelve years since the second world war ended. If my own experience was anything to go on, it would amount to a king's ransom, as the saying goes. Mines, bombs, live shells, rockets, airplanes, and engines—I had dragged up three so far. I had one and know of three other complete double L mine-sweeps that had been recovered in the Thames estuary. Many forty-gallon drums of oil and hundreds of five-gallon drums of paint. Dan-buoys with cable and anchors by the dozen. The list would go on forever.

As so often happens, Fred's loud voice brought me back from my dreams. He wanted to know if I intended getting any sleep today. There was another day tomorrow, not touched yet. This prompted every fisherman in the Ark to move out. We all wanted to see what Val of the Fair-Chance had dragged up in the net!

We had been in the Ark much longer than usual. The tide had dropped so much that Val's weighty object had already started to show above the surface of the water. A crowd of people had gathered to witness the occasion but the interest soon waned as an enormous rock began to appear. The only interesting thing for the spectators to see was several lobsters tangled up in the net. It looked just right for a good big lobster salad to me. Fred said, "Let's get some sleep. You are always thinking about food!"

It was my intention to be out of the harbour as soon as the tide came back. With this in mind we turned in and made the most of what was going to be a six-hour break. This was a good night's sleep when compared with the usual catnaps, Quite a luxury. Before going to sleep, I would make plans for the next day.

It was my intention to try a fresh piece of ground the next day, that is to say, fresh to me. We had never ventured well into the deeper water west of Folkestone Harbour. It was extremely difficult to take marks or depths of water in an effort to explore and be able to return to the same place again. New ground always added an air of mystery to the fishing and this was great! But if I were going to risk gear on rough ground, I needed to know that I could come back to the same area the next day, know exactly where I had been fishing, and reasonably expect to keep clear of trouble.

As I was nodding off to sleep, I wondered if my grandfather had ever come this way, or more likely, my greatuncle George, They were both reputed to be great navigators. Grandfather had been more of a fisherman-cum-pleasure boat skipper. He had skippered the Big Brittania for several years, working from the jetties at Southend-on-Sea every summer. Thousands of people would flock to Southend to sit on the beach and ride on some thirty pleasure boats that worked along the sea-front. It was a tremendous industry.

Uncle George was a totally different cup of tea. He had the notorious reputation of being an out-and-out pirate. All the different characters that I talked with in the early years of my life were of the opinion that he was a loose cannon, but one of the best navigators and fisherman of his day. He appeared to be one of those devils that everyone loved. Eventually I dropped off to sleep. As always, it only needed an unusual sound or movement to wake me. This day, all was quiet.

Both the Paul David and the Dor-Bet motor out of the harbour as the tide comes in. Darkness has descended almost at the same time and it is my plan that we shall venture off to the fresh ground on the next slack tide, at daybreak.

We now have some six hours to fish before that time arrives. I have spoken to Brother Peter and we have agreed that the chance of some large prime plaice and soles across the ranges in the dark is too much of a temptation. We will go down west of the block-ship and gradually work our way back into the ranges. If we can get just one three-hour haul in the shallow water, it could produce a whole night's work. It has got to be worth the risk.

We have just shot the net away inside the block-ship. The Paul David has done the same outside, We are close abreast of each other and will enter the ranges at the same time, but from different angles and without lights. Fred passes a remark under his breath. I pretend not to hear.

Fred prepared us some food and has for the moment disappeared. He is pretending that he is not aware of what is happening or where we are. I am just hoping that he will be able to sleep through the first haul. The deck is ready for the time when we have to start gutting and cleaning. He has three hour's free time, I hope!

As we tow into the ranges, we are only a very short distance apart. There do not appear to be any local boats in the area at all, except maybe for one or two sharpshooters behind the guns, I hope not!

We have towed all the way across the ranges and back past the block-ship without interference of any sort. Fred has slept like a baby the whole time, As we have never caught any amount of small fish on this particular piece of ground, I intend to stay shot as long as possible. The fact that there are no other boats in the area leaves plenty of room to move about on fresh ground. Brother Peter is just on the seaward side of us about a half-mile away. It would appear that he has the same plan in mind.

Fred has just brought me up another cup of tea. He enquires innocently as to where we are. I tell him, "West of the blockship."

He chuckles to himself. "You got away with it then," he shouts. I tell him I won't know until we haul, in twenty minutes' time.

The end chains are on board and we are pulling on the selvages. There is considerable weight but not dead weight, and there are soles and plaice all about the net. Fred gives me a prod in the ribs and says I am a cheeky begger. I *think* he said "begger." The noise of the engine distorts words, it is difficult to tell. Whatever, we have a good day's work in the one haul.

As so often happens when all the best-laid plans appear to be coming to fruition, the sun came up and the fog came down. This is the last thing that I had expected today!

Many a time when I have been working out of Folkestone, great billows of fog have hung around the cliffs but it has stayed clear at sea. Often it has been clear ashore but thick on the water. The fog hangs around in great lumps like the pillar of fire by night and pillar of cloud by day. Whatever, it has shut in very thick at the moment but it does not present us with too much of a problem. I will not venture off on to the fresh ground, as was my intention. We will drop off into eleven fathoms and shoot away towards Dungeness Point in the west.

I have switched on the radio just in case Brother Peter happens to call, which he almost certainly will. There is virtually no shipping likely to come anywhere in our vicinity. The only traffic we have to worry about will be trawlers. I sincerely hope that they will have their radio switched on.

As I expected, Brother Peter called just a few minutes after we had shot away. He also had a very good haul in the dark fishing and was now shot in the eight-fathom line. We would be nicely clear of each other.

Fred was busy gutting and washing the first haul. I would concentrate on keeping us in the right area and also keeping us out of trouble. I decided to give the Fair Chance a call. He did not appear to be switched on yet. Brother Peter called back and suggested that the fog was getting thicker, even dense.

I looked aft. Along the deck where Fred was gutting it really was thick. There was even a haze between us and he was only twenty feet away, content that he had enough fish to keep him busy for the next couple of hours. His old tongue was hanging and he was humming to himself. I could not hear him from where I was sitting in the wheelhouse, but I knew full well that he was humming. I could tell from the painful expression on his face and it was a very painful noise that he made. Nobody would argue with the fact that he was an excellent mate in every way, The Dor-Bet would never be short of gear in any shape or form just so long as Fred was my mate. He was worth his weight in gold.

Storm-force winds and vicious rolling waves are a physical test for any small-boat fisherman. He gets thrown about to a degree that anyone who has not experienced an extended period of this kind of treatment would not understand. Especially when towing a trawl along the sea-bed, the buffeting and the dangers involved are considerable. Fog is a totally different kettle of fish. It is so easy to be lulled into a false sense of security.

I made a point of speaking to Brother Peter (in the Paul David) every fifteen or twenty minutes. Talking to each other on the radio served more than one purpose. It informed other vessels that we were in the area and under way. Each time we discussed our movements it gave them a good idea of our position. I was quite concerned that we had not heard or seen any of the local vessels since we left harbour.

I had just finished speaking to Brother Peter when the Fair-Chance came on the air. Val informed us that he had been round the other side of Dungeness Point in Rye Bay for the dark fishing. It had yielded extremely well for soles but not many plaice. He was now towing east across Hythe Bay towards us. He was also towing in the eleven-fathom line. We would have to be on the lookout for each other.

I informed him that I would move to starboard until the water began to shoal. He acknowledged and said he would keep to the seaward side as he passed, showing us his port bow. I had no idea how far across the bay he had moved but turned to starboard immediately.

I had no sooner put the wheel over than the bow of the Fair-Chance came out of the fog, Visibility could not be any more than twenty-five yards. The two vessels were almost on top of each other but fortunately both moving in a direction that would quickly widen the gap. The two boats would easily avoid a collision but it remained to be seen if our gear would get fouled up or not. We waited for the crunch that never came. Fred shouted, "Bugger me! That was close!" I was still getting my breath back. That was as close as it gets without big trouble.

The Fair-Chance came on the air a few minutes later. "That was a close one, Loll. I'll get you next time." I reply that I will not mind too much if there isn't a next time. It was certainly a near miss!

After coming close to removing some of the paint from the hull of the Fair-Chance, we towed across the bay towards Dungeness for another hour and then hauled.

It was a reasonable haul of mixed fish but the catch continued to be mainly plaice. It was obvious that the season was gradually changing. The fact that we were seeing the odd cod and several whiting each time we towed off into the deeper water was a sure indication that the summer was fast coming to an end.

Here in the Channel winter comes much earlier than in the Thames estuary. We continue to catch skate every day and the satisfying mixture of plaice, lemon soles, grey and spotted dogs, John Dory, crabs and lobsters, and quite a few whelks, which Fred and I love to boil up in the pot and eat hot with a piece of bread and butter. Just the thought of the hot juicy whelks makes me dribble. We shall certainly have some later in the day. They will make a delicious tea.

We have shot away again and are trawling once more towards Folkestone. Providing there are no further hitches, this will be our last haul for today and should bring us back within striking distance of the Harbour.

The fog is persisting and this is rather surprising. I had expected that the strength of the sun would have cleared it away by this time. It is now the middle of the morning. With that little bit of luck which every fisherman needs, we will be landing at midday.

Two hours have quickly passed away and although we have maintained radio contact with the Paul David and the Fair-Chance, we have neither heard or seen any other vessel. I am assuming that most of the local boats have continued to fish west of the point in Rye Bay. At least that is what we are hoping. A dozen vessels going into the harbour at the same time in thick fog, it can get somewhat congested. We are now heaving in on the winch for the last time today.

Our last haul is nothing exceptional but as this is the slack-water time we are not disappointed. There is a good day's pay already boxed up ready for the market, providing that the market prices hold a reasonable level. Some disagree but I have always found Folkestone market to be a very good one. I have informed Brother Peter that we are just jogging towards the harbour in a six-fathom depth of water. We have about forty minutes to go. He is just entering the harbour and the fog appears to be thicker than ever. He had a problem finding the entrance. He jokingly tells me to watch out for the rocks. But it comes mighty close to not being a joke!

Due to the fact that our position east and west is far from certain, it will be necessary for me to do a little bit of guesswork. I know that we are approaching the harbour from a westerly direction and that sooner or later I will have to venture in close to the land in order to establish our exact position. It is possible that we could miss the harbour completely if I delay much longer. I decide to shape in towards the land. I have never seen the fog more dense. I tell Fred to leave the fish for the moment and take up his perch on the forepeak. We shall need to keep a very sharp lookout.

We are heading northeast at our slowest possible speed. The engine is just ticking over and I have a premonition that we are coming close to the land. I can almost smell It. I tell Fred to keep lifting his eyes up as well as forward. I suspect that the fog is thicker on the water than it is in the air.

When the sighting does come, it gives us a bit of a shock to see the high cliffs loom out of thin air above us. I already have the wheel hard to starboard as Fred's huge hand thumps the front of the wheelhouse. The sea-bed comes up on the echo sounder like a vertical pole and I tense my-self for the crunch of rocks on the bottom of the hull, which I feel certain will come any second. I hold my breath as the Dor-Bet comes slowly round to head in the opposite direction. I can hardly believe that we have survived a very close encounter with the land. "The second close shave today," Fred said. "This is becoming a habit! I will need to bring some more clean trousers aboard if you keep frightening the life out of me."

Just as suddenly as the fog shut in it lifted. The harbour stood out clearly just a few minutes' steaming time away to the east. Life could be so easy! Then again it could be so damned hard. Fifteen minutes and we come alongside the slip-way. Brother Peter is waiting for us so that we market both boats' catch at the same time. It would appear that we are the first boats to land, which is unusual. All of the local boats must have ventured round the point into Rye Bay. We will have the Ark all to ourselves!

Brother Peter, Fred, and Arthur had not yet returned from putting our catch on the market. I had finished washing down the decks and was about to go into the wheelhouse and have a wipe around and tidy-up when I noticed an aspiring young fisherman attempting to scull with one oar over the stern of a small skiff. A half-circle groove had been roughly cut into the transom to allow the oar to be shipped. This particular method of sculling is not that easy to master and takes many hours of practice. I watched with interest for several minutes, just to see how he progressed.

I remember the time when I was seven years of age and my grandfather asked me if I wanted to go off to the Reindeer with him. My father and two elder brothers were just washing the catch in preparation for coming ashore. It was laid on the mooring, which was about one hundred yards from the beach. It was my grandfather's intention to give them a hand. He was then semiretired but a very fit, sturdy little man.

He stood with the one oar, sculling right-handed and looking straight ahead. The operation was performed with such skill he made it look so simple, which it certainly was not.

When we came alongside the Reindeer he hopped up onto the deck with an ease which only comes with long experience. He was the first Gilson to be named Yock.

My father told me the story that when my grandfather was still at school he ran errands for one of the local fish shops in Sutton Road. He delivered eggs on a double-ended trade bike every

Saturday morning. On one such morning he was coming down the road at a fair old lick and showing off in front of a group of young ladies when everything went wrong. He fell off the bike and finished up in the middle of the road covered with broken eggs. He was in the habit of speaking with a broad East Essex accent and his first remark was: "Look at all the Yocks." From that time on, all the family became Yocks.

It was four years later that I was allowed to venture out alone and learn to scull. I had mastered the skill and took great delight in showing off my ability along the foreshore on fine summer days. On one of these expeditions I came to grief.

There was a clear stretch of water outside and between two of the jetties that I used for practice. Normally it was clear of any other boats or obstructions but on this day somebody had the nerve to anchor a skiff in the middle of my race course. I was sculling with two hands, intent on building as much speed as possible and lost in my dreams of the future, when there came an almighty crash.

The damage that this caused to the other boat lumbered my father with a whole day's repair work. Naturally I received the customary good hiding and was banned from sculling on my own for several weeks. The wages of sin!

We continued to work out of Folkestone for five more weeks and maintained a reasonable level of fishing most of the time. As the amount of round fish such as cod and whiting increased and became the larger part of the catch, we knew it was time for us to return home to the Thames estuary and prepare for the winter fishing. Our trip down-Channel had been a success. I would be returning home with all my gear intact. This was always something for which I offered up a little word of thanks. It was pointless catching lots of fish if most of the profit was gobbled up paying for new gear. We were now looking forward to all the challenges of another winter, which would soon be upon us.

As usual the Paul David and the Dor-Bet paired up for the winter fishing, both ground trawling and pelagic. Although I was not aware of it at the time, this was going to be Fred's last winter as my mate.

We had a wonderful cod season, taking large catches in very short periods of time with the fish being almost on our doorstep. On one top-tide alone we caught five hundred stone of cod in just six hours' fishing, all prime fish.

Following this, as we came to the beginning of November, sprats began to show on the echo sounder and once again come my birthday on the sixteenth we were into the thick of what turned out to be one of our top seasons. We landed into the three canning factories that we were supplying at the time, seventy-eight thousand bushels of sprats for human consumption. This gave us great satisfaction as none of our family were happy if we had to fish for meal (industrial fishing). Rightly or wrongly we always considered this a waste of valuable stocks.

We had landed six days before Christmas, with all of the boats deep-loaded. This left only six hundred empty boxes on the loading jetty to fulfill our quota.

We had finished unloading at ten P.M. on the Friday night and had completed a full sixteen-hour day. If we were going to fill the last six hundred boxes, they would need to be on the transport and away by midday on the Saturday. We knew this would be tight but we decided to have a go. At four A.M. the following morning the Paul David and the Dor-Bet motored off the Southend shore on the first of the flood tide. In the middle of winter, it would not be daybreak for three hours.

As we deepened the water off the shore, the sprats showed solid on the echo sounder almost from the surface to the sea-bed in ten fathoms of water.

We shot the pelagic trawl, fishing from two fathoms down to a depth of six fathoms. We had the net shot away for no more than eight minutes and it was full. It was four hours later when we landed. It took that long to get them aboard. We had caught far too many.

Ten days later the wind came from the east, bringing with it thick snow and ice and one of the most vicious spells of weather that I ever experienced. We remained in port ice-bound for nine weeks!

Because of the way our family business had developed over the years since the second world war ended, the nine weeks of that bitterly cold winter of continuous ice and snow were not to be wasted. We came together every day to make new nets and repair and put old nets back to their original shape. For me personally one of the most interesting aspects of being a fisherman is designing more efficient nets for the future and this also included larger and more powerful fishing ships to work the gear. It was and I suppose always will be a continuous challenge to most fishermen. It often became a bone of contention among my brothers and myself included as to when a net became too badly damaged to be repaired. With the coming of synthetic materials the nets no longer rotted away but they did often get ripped into many pieces on the numerous wrecks and debris which we regularly retrieved from the sea-bed.

It was at this time that I was given a much more serious problem to take into consideration, a problem that could not have been further from my mind. It had always been my contention that an enthusiastic and capable first mate is one of the essentials in the making of a happy and successful crew on board any fishing ship and this I had always enjoyed with Fred as my friend and right-hand man. This was all coming to an abrupt and very sad end.

In the years that Fred had been working as a fisherman he had had many close encounters with dangerous circumstances that could have ended his life. On two occasions while we worked together on board the Dor-Bet we could have lost the ship in conditions from which there could have been very little chance of survival. Once was due to overloading with fish in what some would call atrocious weather. The second near-miss was due to electrolysis in the hull of the ship, also in strong winds and with a very heavy swell running. We took on board a great deal of water but with all the pumps working full out we managed to survive yet again. The close shaves and near-disasters through close contacts with ships going over the top of our fishing gear and physically pushing us out of the way were too many for comfort. Fred fell overboard on several occasions but always he managed to come back for more. Little did we know that a horrible tumour was growing in his head which would quite bring to an end what had been a very active and vigorous successful life.

Fred had been my friend and partner for several years and the thought of beginning the spring fishing without his loud, rough voice bellowing in my ear above the noise of the wind was unthinkable. Life on board the Dor-Bet would never be quite the same again. The sad and tragic loss of Fred would mark the end of another phase in my most eventful and somewhat hazardous life.

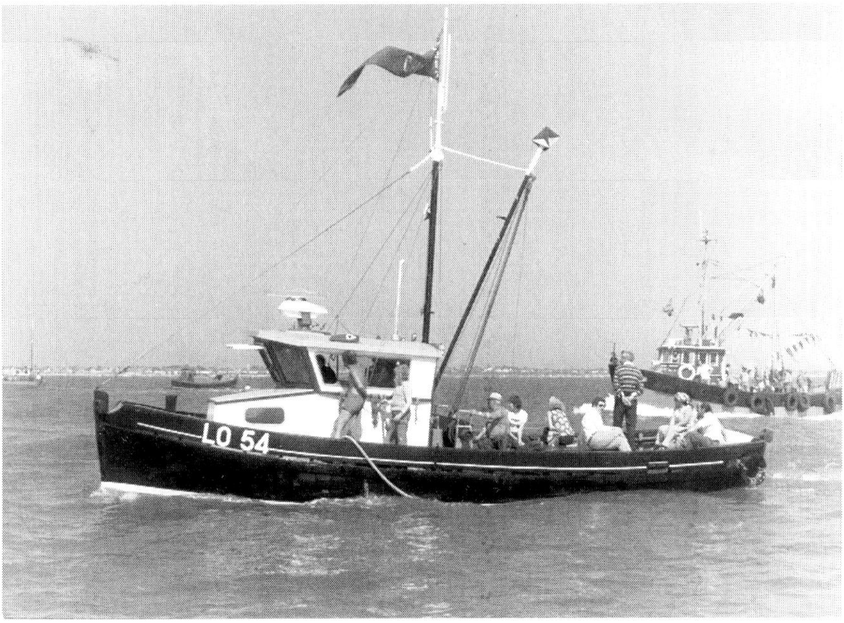
LO 54

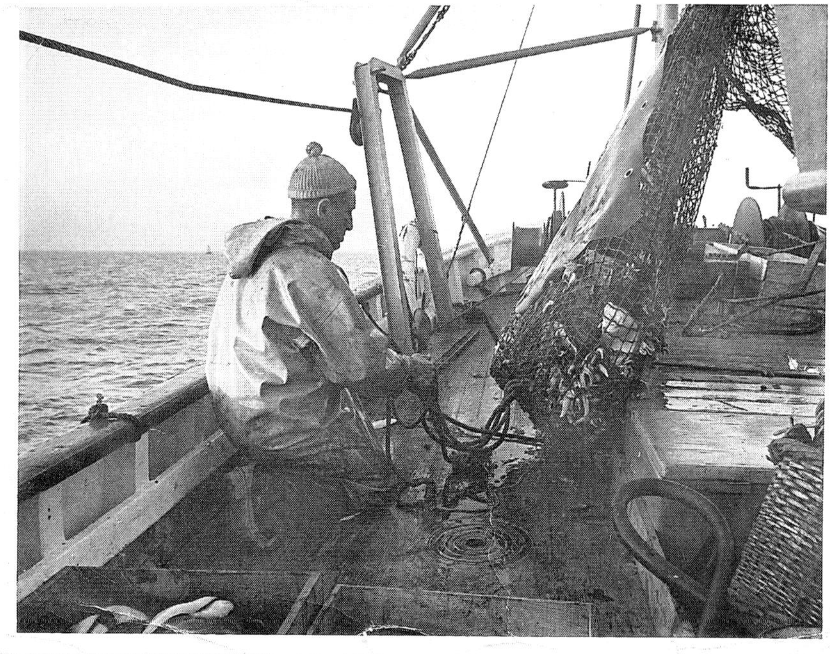

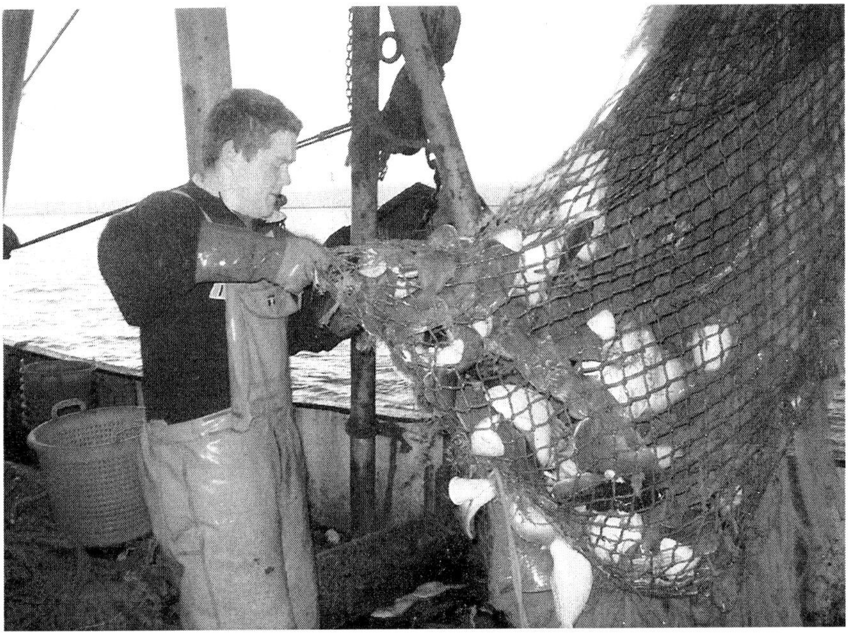

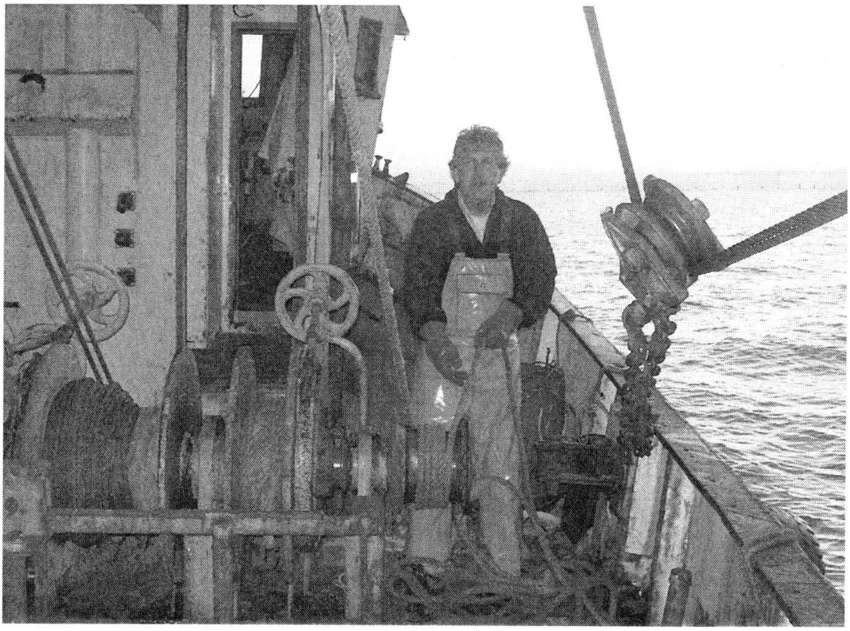